JESUS IN MY GOLF CART

by

Bernita Jackson Brown

Illustrated by Paul Winer

Edited by: Erma Kahle—Wanda Lund

Credits
Unless otherwise noted or paraphrased by the author all
scripture references are from the New King James Version
of the Holy Bible

ISBN: 0-7596-5980-X

This book is printed on acid free paper.

1stBooks – rev. 12/17/01

APPLAUSE FOR-*JESUS IN MY GOLF CART*

I found your manuscript to be **very interesting—** connecting yet hopeful. **Meeting us where we are in the everyday occurrences of life**. Your language and choice of words are not stogy or archaic and the **uninitiated as well as Christians** will find it interesting reading. I commend you in this venture. A strong witness of the gospel.
Rev. Conrad Thompson
Director, Speaker, Lutheran Radio Hour/ Many Years.

A born storyteller, Bernita Brown brings warmth and humor to her writing. She often pokes fun at herself or circumstances in her life in an endearing and disarming way, demonstrating that she is, indeed, human. She relates a believable tale of her efforts to keep Jesus with her in her everyday life - even in her golf cart. Golfers, especially, will know that such an achievement requires constant dedication to spiritual values.
Wanda Lund, Freelance Journalist
Former Staff Writer for Deseret News, Salt Lake City, Utah

A very worthy project of which I wholeheartedly approve. Christians and seekers need this kind of book. Extremely well presented and printed. **Good real-life events and family situations, with a good balance of characters, old and young**. Conversations with Jesus, including the devil's interruptions, all very practical and helpful for a Christians developing life.
Rev. Andrew T. Hughes
Weymouth, Dorser England

Bernita Brown shares with us interesting stories from life that explains explicitly the importance of always taking Jesus with you. She graphically points out in everyday language the importance of not only knowing Jesus but knowing and choosing to walk with him in her daily life. **She shows that one hour a week getting to know Jesus is as insufficient for spiritual health as one meal a week would be for physical maintenance.** She gives evidence that walking with him in faith is the mortar that cements a relationship with him, equips us to be more like him and provides that wonderful sense of 'peace that passes all understanding. **Erma M. Kahle, MS - Speech Communication-Stephen Minister and Bethel Bible Teacher-Bloomington, Illinois**

"We all struggle with taking our faith with us throughout the day, but author, **Bernita Brown, has put her finger right on the problem** with her book "*Jesus in My Golf Cart*". We all mean well on Sunday morning during church service, but applying it to our lives as we rush through chores and family responsibilities is another matter. **Author Brown uses humor as food for thought.** She describes how her busy schedule makes her lose her good intentions, and how Jesus and the Devil vie for her attention. Easy-reading with a nudge to examine our own lives and our relationship with God. **Barbara Taenzler, book reviewer,** *Glenwood Opinion Tribune, Glenwood, Iowa*/**24 years,** *Christian Library Journal.*

TABLE OF CONTENTS

Part II   Is There Life After Golf?

Acknowledgements and Dedication

Emelene Shepherd...*Writer's Digest School* Editorial Staff, who tutored me through my first attempts at writing...**Anita Stanley**...editor of *Water Well Journal* who published the first freelance humor article I ever submitted, launching my self-esteem into orbit.. **Paul Winer** my partner for a second book, who never ceases to amaze me with his delightful illustrations...Most of all special thanks to the Tuesday morning **Writing For Publication group** at Valle del Oro RV Resort in Mesa, Arizona. Each member sat through many re-writes, slashed and trimmed, corrected my grammar and punctuation and still convinced me that this was a viable project. **Wanda Lund, Erma Kahle, Barbara Kimball, Joell Haws, Jim McCarthey, Becky Marshall, Roonie Uhrig and others**, all special friends...What would I do without you?...The **Creative Writer's group** at VDO Resort who for many years have laughed at, encouraged and tolerated my craziness...In addition to those listed above; **Suzie Flock, Verla Holder, Barbara Taenzler, Patrick Johnston, Ellen Brierly, Inez Edwards, Liz Hall, Joy Marie Sheehan, Mary Coutts and many more**,...My **husband Cork**, who has to live with my craziness and put up with me poking fun at him. The **rest of my family** who doesn't always think I'm funny...to my **hometown church**...**Presbyterian Church of Kimball**, in Kimball, Nebraska...To Pastors Norman Austin, Jim George, Mary Bahmer and others, who over the years helped to nourish my faith, once I discovered I had one...And last but not least **Jesus Christ**, who continues to accompany me everywhere I go, trying His best to mold me into the person He wants me to be. A work in progress.

Introduction

It was in Baltimore, Maryland, at the General Assembly of the Presbyterian Church that I first heard the words *"lightly churched."* I came to Baltimore, as a delegate a day early, to attend an evangelism conference. I became interested in evangelism after attending a program in our church called "Covenant For Caring." Being a church member for 30 years didn't qualify me to be a Christian. I was what the speaker called *"lightly churched."*

I felt comfortable with my faith just the way it was, until my grown son started asking questions.

"Mom why does the church believe in the Trinity?"

"Can you explain the Holy Spirit to me?"

"Does it say in your Bible Jesus was born in December?"

"How do we know which Bible translation to believe?"

"Do you consider yourself a Christian?"

"What does it mean to be a Christian?"

Why didn't I keep this kid in Sunday School when he rebelled and didn't want to attend anymore? I go to church whenever I don't have anything else to do. Mostly when it rains and I can't play golf. After all, a person does have to spend time with the family.

I made an attempt at answering his questions. "I don't know about Bible translations? I don't have time to sit around reading different Bibles. Matter of fact I don't read the Bible at all. And the Holy Spirit? A—uh—It's part of the Trinity. I think preachers even have trouble explaining that one."

This incident slowly began to trouble me. Am I a Christian? Do I leave Jesus sitting in the pew on Sunday morning along with my discarded bulletin? And pick him up next month, or two months later when I return for an hour? Is this normal behavior for the average Mr. & Mrs. John Q. Pewsitter in today's church? Is *lightly churched* like lite bread or cookies? Or maybe the *unchurched* are Jesus free like fat free chocolate cake? YUCK!

Does being in church every Sunday make you a Christian? Trying to answer my son's questions created more questions of my own. It gave me the nudge I needed to read the Bible and start attending a Bible study. I felt a need to be more than *lightly churched.*

What would you do if Jesus came to spend a week at your house? *Jesus In My Golf Cart* is fiction but based on my true feelings. In no way do my words express the views of any religion or denomination. Any resemblence to persons, places or things are purely intentional. Some names have been changed to keep me from being sued. Come along for the ride of your life as I bring Jesus home to spend a week with me.

Chapter One

TAKE JESUS WITH YOU

One sun-shiny Sunday morning I sit in church gazing out the window, watching the thin ribbons of clouds lacing the sky. The spicy fragrance of newly mown grass drifts in through the open window. I can't help thinking of the many unfinished projects waiting for me at home. Most of all I have a golf date at 1pm and am worried about the pastor talking too long.

"If you have accepted Jesus as your Savior and invited Him into your life, you won't leave Him in the pickup truck while you walk into a bar, or anyplace else to have a good time," the pastor says. "You will want to take Him with you wherever you go."

I shift into an alert mode and attentively listen to the rest of the sermon. What if I try our pastor's suggestion and take Jesus home with me? Is it possible Jesus can help me cope in a world as crazy as mine? Then it dawns on me that if I claim to be a Christian this is what I'm supposed to do. I ponder a while before making up my mind to take Jesus with me through one of my busy weeks. If at the end of the week my life isn't changed, I tell myself, I'll bring him back next Sunday.

I rush Jesus along after church, explaining to him that we have a golf date and it's best if we don't stay for coffee and visiting.

"Don't you enjoy staying after church and getting to know more of the people?" He asks. "Maybe some are hurting. There may be something you can do to comfort them. Others may need help to celebrate a happy occasion."

"If I ask the older people how they are, I have to listen for 30 minutes while they explain everything that aches and throbs. I'm too busy for that today. We'll do it next week," I say, as Jesus and I rush for the car.

As we're driving along I remember that my house is dirty and I haven't even thought about what I'm going to serve for a quick lunch. And what about my husband, Cork? Maybe I shouldn't jump into this experiment without thinking. Oh, well, it's too late now. Wait until I tell Cork what I'm doing. He'll know for sure I've flipped my lid this time. Maybe I can keep it a secret for a while, I thought.

"Your mind is preoccupied with worries. Can I help you in any way?" Jesus asks.

"No, not now, maybe later."

I quickly stir up a tuna salad and throw bread and corn chips on the table. We never have prayed at meal time and I don't have time to try and stumble through a prayer now. Feeling uncomfortable, I start eating. Jesus takes time to bow his head and silently thank His Father for the food.

"Dear, will you mind clearing off the table? I'll be late for my tee time," I ask, as Jesus and I run out the door.

"Your husband doesn't know me. Why didn't you introduce me to him?"

"I will later. We don't have time to get into a deep conversation on why you're here. He may not understand."

When we arrive at the golf course I have to make a decision. Will there be room in the golf cart for Jesus? I give Him a choice: He can sit in the middle between my partner, Pat, and me, or He can walk. He chooses to sit in the middle. Do I tell Pat Jesus is here? What if she sits on His lap or steps on His robe? I don't tell her because I don't want her to think I'm one of those "religious" ones.

We make a pretty picture tooling down the fairway in my old rickety, purple golf cart with a bumper sticker reading "Golf Is For Lovers." Jesus is scrunched in the middle with an arm around each of us. I start to get jealous, but Jesus doesn't give me a chance. **"I love both of you,"** He says.

When I jump out of the cart, Jesus does too. I wonder if it will be proper to ask for help with my game. It's worth a try.

"Instead of just standing there, why don't you hold your hand on my right shoulder so I don't dip down and hit the ground?" I ask.

"First you need to learn how to relax and enjoy yourself. You've rushed around all morning and are tighter than a harp string. You can't swing a golf club with stiff shoulders. Try it again."

As I'm swinging, I feel Jesus' hand on my shoulder and I have a super shot. So I share this with my friends.

"Think of some good looking guy holding your shoulder back," I say. Of course I don't tell them about Jesus.

I can't resist mentioning to Jesus that I've never had a hole in one, and if He feels like performing miracles, this will be a good time. He acts like He doesn't hear me.

Suddenly I look around and there's Jesus riding in the cart with the other two girls in our foursome. He is sitting in the middle with an arm around each of them. I holler across the fairway.

"What are you doing? They don't even know you're here."

Jesus looks at me with a gentle, compassionate smile and says, **"You don't know that for sure."**

He's right. I don't know. I haven't ever talked to my friends about Him. I start to tighten up again and when I take a fast, jerky swing the ball heads right for Barracuda Lake.

"I've heard you can walk on water. Any chance you can retrieve my ball from the middle of the lake? That was a new one. They cost $3 apiece." When I turn around Jesus is gone.

I can see it's going to be a day of learning for me as Jesus goes cart-hopping all over the course.

Chapter Two

TWO NEW FRIENDS

Monday morning at 5:30 the dull buzz of the alarm clock wakes me from a deep sleep. I lay there dreaming about a tall, dark, good-looking guy holding his hand on my shoulder as I take a hefty swing at a golf ball.

Slowly coming to my senses, I remember it's Jesus I'm dreaming about. This is the second day of my week-long adventure of taking Jesus with me.

"Hope you can keep up," I say to Jesus as I slowly drag myself out of bed.

"Can we take time for prayer to start the day?" Jesus asks.

"You go ahead. I'll pray while I'm in the shower."

"Singing in the rain, just singing in the rain," I sing as I shampoo my hair. The sign on the shower head reminds me it's my day to examine my breasts. I'll have to examine and pray at the same time.

"Dear God, I want to get to know Jesus. If there's any way I can work Him into my life—show me where and how. I want to be a better Christian. That's all I have time for now. Amen."

Every Monday during the summer I play golf with a group of senior ladies at different courses around the western part of Nebraska. This is one time I'm glad 55 is old enough, especially when it comes to competing in golf. I started the summer thinking I had a chance to win, but so far no accolades came my way.

Tee time today is at 10am in Mitchell, Nebraska. Monday is also the day I reserve for working in the office. I get a head start on month-end work by filling out invoices once a week. If I hurry I can have them ready for approval before our 8 o'clock departure. Our home-based business of drilling and repairing water wells provides us with a good living. It also keeps Cork and I, and two sons, busier than a hive of bees in the summer.

By 6:30 I have my shower, coffee brewing and cereal on the table, ready for my husband who is finishing his morning shave. I sit down to enjoy a cup of coffee while waiting.

"Are we going to have time to visit your Aunt in the Manor today?" Jesus asks.

"Maybe. I'll see what time we arrive home from Mitchell."

My husband, Cork greets me with instructions about invoices that need finished before I leave for golf.

"Yes, Dear. I know. I'll be done before I leave town."

I give him a quick peck on the cheek before starting my task. As soon as Cork leaves for work I dash to the basement and start a load of laundry. The telephone rings three times. I write down work orders for the day and hang up quickly on two salesmen. My sister, Carol, calls with a long story about her night of agonizing pain. The doctor won't listen to her complaints and I don't have time.

I glance at my watch and see there is only time to gather my golf equipment, two layers of clothes, water jug and cooler for fruit and snacks. The weather changes so often in Nebraska you have to be prepared for anything. Thank God I'm not driving today. I'll be the last one on the route to pick up. My shoes will have to go unpolished again. Maybe there will be time to check on my sister later.

"Jesus are you sure you want to come along on this trip?"

"I wouldn't miss it. I want to see what your priorities are."

Arriving in Mitchell, we unload the golf equipment and head for the pro shop. We called three days ahead and were already paired according to handicap for a two-person scramble. The pairings are made with a high and a low handicap woman playing as a team. I pay my fee and find my golf cart. I don't recognize the name of the lady who is my partner. I wait around the cart until it's time to leave for the 1st tee. Then I dash back into the pro shop to find my partner and almost run over a little lady with a hump on her back, toting an oxygen tank.

"I'm sorry," I say as I holler at the pro to help find my partner.

"You're looking at her," was his answer, as the heavy-breathing, spindly, little lady proceeded to my cart.

My drooping chin and bugging eyes may have given my feelings away. You have to be kidding, I thought.

"Get out there and play good golf today. You have a big handicap to overcome," the pro said.

"Jesus, where are you? How am I going to handle this one? I'm going to need a miracle today."

I try to smile and introduce myself to Marj. Then I feel Jesus' hand on my shoulder. A calmness comes over me and I feel relaxed for the first time in days.

"Just keep your cool. This lady wants to play golf with you. Marj had polio when she was young. She struggles for every breath she takes. She needs you to help her feel comfortable with her game. No matter what happens, be nice to her and make her feel welcome. Can you do that for me?" Jesus asked.

"Yes, Jesus, with your help I'll try. After all, winning isn't everything."

I know the local girls gave Marj to me because they didn't want her on their team. Reading my thoughts Jesus responds.

"No, Bernita, the chairman gave Marj to you because she knows you will be nice to her. She knows you can handle the situation gracefully. She knows you are a Christian and are willing to help me. Each time you do something for the least of these brothers and sisters of mine you do it for me," Jesus whispers.

"Are you the Brown that wrote the Snowbird book about senior citizens going to Arizona for the winter in their RV's?" Marj asks.

"I sure am. Have you heard about my book?"

"I've read it. Friends from Casper, Wyoming, Andrew and Marilyn Jackson, loaned it to me. I like it so well I want my own copy. Where can I buy it?"

My mouth fell open again.

"Andrew Jackson's my cousin. How do you know him?"

Our conversation continues on the way to the first tee box.

I learn about Marj's polio and her never give up attitude. I admire her because she never complains. She apologizes several times because she can't hit the ball very far.

A two-person scramble is when both players hit each shot, take the best ball and hit again. The team only has one score. I deliver her to the ball each time so she doesn't have far to walk.

"I'll drive the ball, you help with putting and chipping," I tell Marj when she shows signs of tiring. When we arrive at the green I line her up and tell her where to putt the ball. Surprisingly, she does what I say. She sinks the putts and I don't have to try. I forget about winning, relax and have a great time.

When it's time to award the prizes, I am amazed when we come in second. Nobody cheers louder than we do. We both earn a $40 credit at the pro shop. Marj and I have a grand time spending our money. I buy Jesus and me a tee shirt. Mine reads "Golf Is For Lovers." Jesus' shirt reads "God's Love Is For All."

That night I fall into bed exhausted. I immediately fold my hands and pray.

"Dear God, thank you for giving me the chance to get to know Jesus better. Please forgive me for my sinfull thoughts and deeds. I will try to do better. I feel good about making friends with Marj today. Please bless her and continue to watch over her. If you have any other jobs I can help you with just let me know. Amen."

Chapter Three

PRAISE THE LORD

Tuesday morning I bounce out of bed before the alarm. Five hours of sleep and I feel like a new person. Today I may be able to hit the ball 200 yards and sink all my putts, I think to myself.

"Good morning Jesus. Bless everyone I love," I say, as I walk through the house to raise the shades and brighten my world.

"Good morning, Bernita. Do we have time for prayer this morning? There are others who need God's blessing today, too."

While I contemplate my answer, the telephone rings.

"Good morning," I say in my most pleasant voice.

11

"Collect call from LaWanda. Will you accept the charges?" the operator asks.

"Yes, I guess so," I answer.

"Aunt Bernita, It's me. How is everything with you today?" She asks.

"You're calling pretty early in the morning is something wrong?"

"Not too much. Mom doesn't feel good and we don't have any food in the house. It's a week until her check comes. Can you send us $20? We need gas so I can take Mom to the doctor too," LaWanda pleads.

"Are you driving without a license? Have you been going to school LaWanda?"

"No."

"Have you thought about finding a job?"

"The car isn't running very good and I can't get back and forth to town."

"Where's Mary? Can she come to the phone?"

I talk to my sister, Mary, who lives in Missouri. She's having trouble keeping her blood sugar regulated and it's making her feel badly. She's a single mother, living off of welfare because she's too sick to work. She has a 15 year old daughter who thinks she's 21. My brother, Dale, lives near them. Mary and LaWanda live in one of his rental houses. Dale is single, retired, and tired of helping. He also runs out of money before the end of the month.

"I have a lump in my breast. I think it's growing. I haven't been to the doctor because I can't afford it," Mary says.

"Mary for *crissake* get to the doctor! How long have you had the lump?"

"Oh, I don't know. Probably six months or more," she cried.

12

"Why in the world didn't you say something before this? I can't be there to take you to the doctor. You may have cancer!" I shrieked. "I'm sure Dale will take you if you call him. I'll send money today. How much do you think you'll need?"

"If you can spare $50, I'll pay you back when my check comes," she answers.

"Now what do they need money for?" Cork wants to know as he pauses at the door on his way to work.

"The usual. No food in the house. But, now Mary has a lump in her breast and hasn't been to the doctor with it. I can't understand anyone that won't visit the doctor when they have a lump. It's pure ignorance," I exclaim.

"Sounds like another ploy to get you to send money," Cork answers. "By the way, I can't find the invoices you were working on yesterday. Be sure and have them for me tonight. Bye"

"We need to talk about this later," I tell Jesus. "Our tee time is at 8:00. We have to go now."

The phone rings again. It's my sister, Carol.

"Can you come down? I really need to talk to someone. I'm having so much pain. Please," she sobs.

"I can't come right now, but will be there right after lunch," I tell her.

"Carol calls every day with the same complaints. I never know if she's really sick," I tell Jesus.

The phone rings again before He can answer me. It's my mother.

"Dad and Carol both need a haircut, can you do it today? she asks.

"I'm late for golf right now. I'll be down after lunch. Can you walk over to Carol's and see if she's all right? Thanks, Mom. See you this afternoon."

13

Tuesday mornings I play golf with a group of fun ladies. We draw for partners and have a different foursome every week. I feel like I need to play to keep my swing grooved for the Nebraska Women's Amateur Golf tourney we're hosting next week. I'm paired with a friendly bunch of girls, but two of them haven't played very much golf. We spend a great deal of time waiting. Jesus is resting under a tree. My thoughts are wandering. I should have stayed home, checked on Carol and wired Mary the money. The dreaded invoices aren't made out either.

"Oh! Good God!" Polly exclaims, as she takes a hefty swing and misses the golf ball.

"Yes, He is good isn't He," comes a deep voice from under the tree.

"Who said that?" she asked, looking around.

"I did," I say, holding my throat. "My voice is hoarse."

"I wish I'd thought of that," I told Jesus. "Why don't you give the girls a few tips on their game? We have other things to do besides sit out here all day."

"You know more about golf than I do," he answers. **"You tell them, I'll help."**

"Think about Jesus holding your shoulder back, so you don't dip down and hit the ground." I tell Polly.

"Jesus! What good can He do? I need someone closer than that,"comes the reply.

"Just try it once and see. You do know Jesus, don't you?"

"You mean Jesus Christ? With the beard, sandals and white robe?"

"Yeah, God's Son. Try it."

"Oh, sure, I know Jesus, but I never thought about asking Him to help with my golf game." Polly takes a graceful swing and hits the ball 150 yards.

"Hallelujah! it works," she exclaims, hopping down the fairway like a rabbit and shouting with joy.

"I'm going to try that too," Donna says, as she approaches the lake near the #13 hole. "If I make it over it'll be the first time this year." She takes a jerky swing and smashes the ball into the lake. It glances off the water three times and bounces onto the green three feet from the hole.

Donna raises her arms in the air and falls to her knees. "Praise the Lord!" she exclaims.

Jesus turns to me and says, "**See how easy it is to share your faith with your friends. Look, both of them are praising God.**"

Chapter Four

SATAN RIDES ALONG

After finishing my round of golf and sharing a salad luncheon at the club house, Jesus and I head for the grocery store. I plan to pick up a few groceries and wire money to Mary.

On the two mile ride into town I start thinking about how much to send. LaWanda said $20 and Mary asked for $50. They don't have any gas, the cars not running right, Mary needs to see a doctor and the cupboard's bare. After mulling it over I decide $50 will be sufficient.

"Do you want my opinion?" Jesus asks.

"Oh. Sure. I'm sorry. I get lost in my thoughts and forget you're here. What do you think I should send?"

"Is it possible Mary and her daughter need other things? On a trip to town they may want to stop at a restaurant. Can you spare enough so the girls can have a special treat? If your brother has to drive them, he will need a meal too. Can you understand why Dale might be tired of helping them? Personal items are expensive. One hundred dollars should cover any thing they may need, today" Jesus adds.

"Whoa! Whoa! Whoa!" came a voice from the back seat, "Why should she be concerned with special treats and personal items? She has her own needs to think about."

"Who is that?" I cry out, looking around and almost driving into the ditch.

"It's Beelzebub," Jesus answers.

"I don't see anybody. Do you have other friends here? I don't remember agreeing to take anyone else with me this week."

"I call Satan, 'Beelzebub,' or Bub. He's always here. He sits around waiting to pounce on anyone that will listen," Jesus said.

"Maybe he has a point. I hardly ever get paid back when I send Mary money. That's why I don't send very much."

"She has nothing. You have more than you need. One of the main requirements for being a Christian is to share what you have," Jesus said. **"Remember, whatever you do for the least of these brothers and sisters of mine you do for me."**

"How do you know they'll spend the money on necessary things?" Bub wants to know. "Mary's probably out of cigarettes. Do you really think cigarettes are a necessary item? Her daughter wastes money on junk food

18

and running with her friends. I say don't send them anything. We can use that money to have a good time."

I feel Jesus' hand on my shoulder again. The warmth and peace that envelops me is indescribable.

"It's not your place to worry about how the money is spent, or if you'll ever get it back. My Father will see to that," Jesus whispers.

"I'll have to be a tightwad this month if I send $100. I suppose I can get along with one less trip to the mall. Get behind me, Bub, and keep your comments to yourself. I've decided to send $100."

Driving on with eyes open, I pray.

"Jesus, please forgive me. I know Mary and LaWanda will appreciate a special treat on us. I'm sorry about using your name loosely this morning when talking to Mary."

Jesus' hand remained on my shoulder as he counseled me.

"Remember you can talk to me anytime. You have a tendency to hold your worries inside and try to solve everyone's problems yourself. So far this week the only thing you've asked me to do is help with your golf game. I want to be first in your life. I want to go with you. I want to be your friend, comforter and enabler. I want to slowly teach you and mold you into a Christian, one small step at a time. Please don't leave me riding in the back seat of your life, with Bub."

"OK Jesus. It feels good knowing you are here with me, but I can see it's not going to be easy and it won't happen overnight. Please be patient with me.

Chapter Five

SATAN RIDES ALONG-PART ll

After the money is sent, I travel back across town to our home and office. I need to check the answering machine and see which job needs my attention first.

I no more than walk into the kitchen when I hear the guys talking on the radio. "KNBE-640, Unit one to base." I hurry to pick up the mike.

"This is the base. Go ahead."

"I'm 25 miles north of town and need you to bring out a 1-horsepower pump. It will save us about an hour. We need a 10EJ10. Can you bring it?" Cork asks.

"I'm going to check on Carol first. Then I'll be right out. I should be there in 30 minutes."

"OK, but don't dally. We need the pump now. Did the sand and gravel truck arrive yet? I left a note on the answering machine. Check that out before you leave town."

"10-4. I'll have my cellular phone along if you need to contact me again. Bye."

I hang up and push the button to listen to the morning messages. There is a message from Carol. She's feeling better so I don't have to hurry. One grandson needs picked up from pre-school and one from kindergarten. The load of gravel will arrive sharply at 2pm. Driver needs someone at the shop to show the truck where to dump. Customer 30 miles north is out of water.

"I don't know when I'll finish making out invoices," I say to Jesus as we run down the basement steps two at a time. Half way down I stumble on Jesus' robe and we end up in a pile at the foot of the stairs. He picks me up and we continue through the garage and into the van for a busy afternoon.

"First, we'll gather up Preston from pre-school, then travel crosstown to wait the arrival of the gravel truck. With any luck at all we'll be back here when kindergarten lets out. Don't let me forget to pick up the pump."

"Why don't you stop and check on your sister?" Jesus asks. **It might be good for her to get out for some fresh air. She can ride with us."**

"Sounds to me like we have a load already," Bub answers loudly. "Cork will be mad if we're late. Besides, all she does is moan and groan and complain. Leave her home!"

"I'll give Carol a quick call. If she can be ready in five minutes I'll pick her up on the way."

We pick Carol up, oxygen tank and all and arrive at pre-school with two minutes to spare. We wait and wait

21

and no Preston. Finally I jump out of the car and run to the door.

"You're waiting at the wrong door, Gramma," three year old Preston informs me. "You're s'posed to pick me up at the back door in the alley."

"I'm sorry. Gramma didn't know. We'll get it right next time. Let's go. We're running late. Everybody buckle up."

We speed to the West side of town in time to show the driver of the gravel truck where to unload. I unlock the shop and start to load a pump into the back of the van.

"That's the wrong size pump," Beelzebub hollers through the window. "Your husband asked for a 1-1/2hp, or was it just a 1/2hp?"

"Gramma, I have to potty," Preston says.

"Don't you know which pump he asked for?" Carol asks.

"Take the brat to the pot before he makes a mess," Bub adds.

"I need a cola. Do you have any in there?" Carol wants to know.

"Be calm," Jesus counsels as his hand returns to my shoulder.

I send Preston to the bathroom and grab Carol a diet cola from the frig. I know with her diabetes she is always thirsty. Then I load three pumps because I can't remember which size to take. I throw in control boxes and pressure switches to match each pump, just in case they're needed.

"Cork's not going to like your messing around," Bub tells me. "We might as well stop downtown and go shopping!"

All loaded and ready to travel again, we drive back to the West Elementary School. Mitchell is waiting for us when we drive up.

"Hi, Mitch, did you have a good day?" I ask.

"No, the teacher made us take a nap. I'm too old for naps. Gramma, can we stop at the Dairy Queen for a snack?"

"We can't right now, Mitch," I answer, "but we will after a ride in the country."

Right away Beelzebub makes his presence known. "Are you going to let these little brats starve? Can't you let them off at home? They can find their own snack. I don't want them in the same car with me."

"Gramma, why does Carol have a cola? I want one," Preston complains.

Mitchell and Preston gather up small pillows and start having a fight. It's not long until polyester and sponge particles start flying all over the van.

"It's Bub," Jesus assures me, as my blood pressure starts rising. **"He's up to his usual tricks. Don't pay any attention to him."**

"Is everyone buckled up? We'll be back in town in half an hour. Then we'll all have a treat," I tell them.

Thirty minutes later we arrive at our destination.

"What held you up?" my impatient husband asks. "We have other people out of water." I tried to call and you didn't answer."

"Oh, we've just been joy riding," I answer. "By the way, the Andersons five miles further north are out of water, too. I brought extra pumps in case you need another."

"Thanks for bringing the pumps and parts. We'll go on to Andersons from here. Don't forget the invoices I need tonight."

Arriving back in town, we stop for ice cream cones.

"I want confetti sprinkles on mine," Preston says.

"I want a large, double hot fudge sundae," Bub adds.

"I want hot fudge with whipped cream on it." Mitchell says.

"I'll have a hot, double fudge peanut buster parfait," Carol chimes in.

"Carol, you know you can't eat all that sugar. We're only having cones. No hot fudge. I have to watch my pennies and calories this month," I say, as my mouth starts watering.

"One of Bub's tricks is to whet your appetite with goodies you shouldn't have. You always have to be on guard for his suggestions." Jesus continues to educate me about His continual pain in the neck.

If Preston's having confetti sprinkles, I want chocolate sprinkles," says Mitchell.

"I'll have another diet cola," Carol adds.

Finally getting everyone satisfied with treats, we take Carol home.

"Thanks for letting me ride along. I feel better now," Carol says as she exits the van.

"Tell Dad I'll be by tomorrow to give hair cuts," I tell Carol. I really need to go home and finish making out statements, before I lose my job. I'm glad you came with us. Bye now."

Arriving back home, I get the boys started playing in the sand pile with cars and trucks.

"Gramma, it's my turn to bring treats tomorrow. Can we help you make cookies?" Preston asks.

"Are you sure?"

"Yup. I have a note in my pocket."

Checking out his pockets, I find the note. Our son Jerry, is divorced and has physical custody of the boys. I try to help him whenever I can. If Preston needs treats tomorrow I had better bake something.

"Will it be OK if we just put frosting between graham crackers?" I ask.

"That'll be good Gramma. I like graham cracker cookies."

"I want you to make us a candy bar," Mitchell says.

"I really don't have time, Mitchell. Gramma has work to do in the office."

I feel Jesus near and stop to listen as his hand on my shoulder quiets me.

"Take this time to be with your grandchildren. Hold them, read to them, make cookies or play with them. Take every opportunity you can to tell them about me. I know the two boys are very special to you. Their mother isn't always around. They need this time with you. Children grow up too fast. You can work in the office later tonight."

I decide to do what Jesus suggests. I spend about an hour putting together makeshift cookies and creating my famous peanut butter candy bars. The boys are settled into the sand box again and I run to the basement to throw in another load of laundry.

"You should be in the office working or you'll be in trouble again tonight," Bub says. The kids are fine. They can play by themselves. If you have any of that peanut butter candy left you better have some while you have a chance. You know when Jerry and Cork get home they'll finish it off and you won't even get a taste. By the way, what are you fixing for supper?"

Going back upstairs, I help myself to a large piece of candy and head for the office. I start going through today's mail and begin on a customer's statement when I hear crying from outside.

"Gramma, Mitchell's throwing sand down my neck," Preston cries.

"The devil made me do it," Mitchell answers.

"I can believe that. Mitchell, please be good Gramma has work to do."

Calming that storm, I return to the office.

"Gramma, come and see what Mitchell did," I hear five minutes later.

"OK, I'll come and look in a minute."

Knowing that I might as well give up trying to do office work, I grab the trash and go out the back door onto the patio.

"Hurry Gramma," Mitchell says, jumping up and down.

"You boys need to learn to be patient. As soon as I empty the trash I'll be right there."

I stop to pull a few weeds in the garden and slowly amble towards the front of the house.

"Gramma, you better hurry!" Preston says, as he runs to meet me.

"Oh! No!" I scream, as I round the corner of the house to find Mitchell jumping up and down, clapping his hands and laughing. The lawn sprinkler sits on the front porch wetting down the picture window and soaking the carpet through the open front door.

"You little brats! I'm going to spank your bottoms," I holler, as the boys high tail it around the side of the house.

"It's not their fault," Jesus says, as I feel his hand on my shoulder again. **Bub is up to his old tricks. Don't be too hard on the boys. They are precious in my sight."**

"OK, but I've had it with Beelzebub," I state emphatically.

"I wanted you to know how much trouble Bub can cause. You have to remember he will come back whenever he feels I'm making any headway in your life."

"Thank you, Jesus. Please forgive me for calling my grandsons brats. They are very special to me too."

When Cork and Jerry arrive home they sense that I am frazzled. "How about ordering pizza for supper tonight?" Jerry asks. "I'll go pick it up while you fix the drinks and salad. Then the boys and I can go home and get ready for bed and another day of school and work."

When the house is quiet Cork suggests we watch a movie and forget making out invoices until later.

"Thanks for understanding. It has been a challenging day," I tell him, as I curl up on the couch with his arm around me.

Chapter Six

YOUR LIFE IS LIKE AN UNMADE BED

I groan and turn over in bed when the alarm goes off at 7am on Wednesday morning. Cork turns off the alarm and starts his morning chores. He whistles a tune along with the noisy bird songs floating through the open window. How can they be so happy this early in the morning. I can't get up. I'll lay here a few minutes longer, I think to myself.

The next thing I know it's 9am and the phone is ringing. I grab the phone to hear Carol's voice on the other end.

"It's time to get up. What time are you coming down to cut hair?"

"I have to make out invoices first. I'll be down around 11," I tell her.

I drag myself out of bed and head for the shower. I don't know why I didn't get up at 6:30 like I usually do. It makes me feel worse to sleep so long.

"You needed the extra sleep," Jesus said. "Your body is a temple. God wants you to take care of yourself as well as others. I hope you have time for prayer this morning."

"Oh, Jesus. I keep forgetting you're here. "I'll pray as soon as I get my shower," I answer.

I rush through the shower washing my hair, knowing it will take an extra thirty minutes to dry and curl. Too many days of golf, sun and neglect have it looking like a dust mop. I should file my nails and deep clean my face but I can't take the time. I have a golf date at 2pm and a hundred things to do before that. After dressing I start making the bed when Jesus reminds me we need to talk.

"Your life is like an unmade bed," Jesus says. **"It's wrinkled and disheveled. Leave the bed unmade each day until you take time to pray. Every time you walk by you will remember. Then as you smooth out the sheets and blankets let God help smooth out your life. Let Him comfort you as he warms and lifts you to start each day."** We kneel beside the bed and Jesus' hand returns to my shoulder.

"Dear God, "I know my life is a mess. I'm trying to learn. I'm so mixed up. I have to help care for my family. I'm always running behind. I don't have enough time today to finish what I started yesterday."

"Father please forgive me," I do need your help. My sister Mary, is going to the doctor with a lump in her breast. Please don't let it be cancer. Watch over her and LaWanda.

My sister Carol is ill too. Please ease her pain. My sisters don't really know you and I-I- guess I don't either. What can I do? Please watch over my family at work and play and show me today what to do first. I know I need to tell my family about Jesus, but I don't feel comfortable doing it. I don't know what to say. Can you help me Lord? Amen."

With Jesus' hand on my shoulder I feel relaxed.

"Everything will work out for good for those who love me." Jesus counsels. "Sometimes God does things different than we expect. Our prayers aren't always answered immediately. The gift of life everlasting and the seeds of my love have been planted within you. The seed will grow and blossom until your heart bursts with joy. Then you will know for sure you want to be one of my followers and take me with you forever."

By 10 am I'm in the office preparing a deposit to take to the bank. I also need to stop at the postoffice for stamps, the courthouse to license a truck and drop checks off to pay the monthly utility bills. While I'm making out the checks Cork drives into the yard in the truck.

"Do you have the invoices done yet?" he shouts in the back door. "Come here I have something for you."

"Oh, what a cute little puppy. Where did he come from?"

"She's yours. A farmer gave her to me. I knew you would be tickled to have another puppy. She's a Cocker Spaniel. I've missed Muffin terribly. Aren't you excited.?"

"No! I'm not excited. She's cute to look at, but I'm having trouble taking care of the people in my life without adding a baby. Please take her back where you got her."

"I can't. I have to get back to work. See you at noon for lunch. Don't let her get cold," he says, as the pup squats and wets on my kitchen carpet. I grab her and head for the garage where I find a big box.

Beelzebub nudges me and says, "What are we going to do with a pup? Now you'll have to feed her? Leave her out here in the cold garage. She's going to make a mess. You'll never get to the golf course today."

"I thought you were gone. Just leave me alone. I don't have time for you." I take the box and dog into the basement and run back up the stairs to the office. Thirty minutes later I have the checks written out and the deposit ready. Maybe I'll have time to make out invoices after golf.

I arrive at Carol's and find her soaking her feet. I cut her toe nails every two weeks. Carol has diabetes and poor circulation. We have to be careful not to cut too deep and cause a sore on her feet.

"Why do you have to do this? She could cut her own toe nails if she wasn't so fat. If she'd get off her duff and move we'd all feel better," Bub announces.

I decide to ignore the little devil and see if he disappears. After cutting Carol's nails and hair I walk on around the block to my Mother and Dad's apartment. Dad is happy to see me and talks constantly while I cut his hair.

"He's lonely," Jesus whispers.

33

"Why don't you stay and have lunch with us?" Dad wants to know.

"Cork is coming home for lunch today. I better go on home as soon as I run a few errands downtown. He brought a puppy home for me to care for. He didn't think I had enough to keep me busy. I'll have lunch with you another day. OK?"

"We have six kids, ten grandkids and twenty great grandkids and none of them have time to visit. We can sit here and rot and nobody will care," my Mother says.

"I promise as soon as I catch up in the office I'll spend more time with you. See you soon," I add, as I run for the car.

By this time it's twelve o'clock. I head for home instead of running errands.

"See, how my day goes," I say to Jesus. No matter what I do there's always somebody that's not happy."

"Seems to me like you should take more time for yourself and forget everybody," Bub announces. "Why can't your sister and Dad go to the beauty shop for their haircuts? I'm tired of this messing around. Let's drive on out to the golf course and practice before tee time. We can have a sandwich out there. Let your husband fix his own lunch and take care of that pup."

"I'm tempted," I answer, but Jesus' hand on my shoulder allows me to ignore Bub and think about lunch. My brain is trying to scan the contents of the refrigerator for lunch possibilities. I remember there's a bowl of leftover stew in the freezer. I can thaw it quickly in the microwave.

Driving into the yard I arrive at the same time as Cork and Mike.

"Jerry's coming too," Mike says, getting out of the pickup. We need to have a meeting. I tried to call, but can't ever catch you at home."

I open the garage door to the sounds of a crying puppy.

"Cork take care of your dog if you expect me to fix lunch." Realizing the stew won't go all the way around I start making grilled cheese and ham sandwiches only to find there isn't enough cheese or bread to feed everyone.

"Bring the bread and cheese to me, " Jesus says. **"Have everyone sit down."** I watch in amazement as Jesus looking up to heaven blesses and breaks the bread and hands it back to me. There is more bread than when I handed it to him. He does the same thing with the cheese. Standing with my mouth open I can't believe what I see.

"I've heard you can multiply bread, but I never expected it to happen right here in my kitchen." You really are Jesus, the Christ aren't you?"

"Yes I Am," Jesus replies. **"I'm sorry your family doesn't know me. Can you introduce them to me now?"**

"I'd like to wait a little longer until I feel more comfortable talking about you. Can I have more time?" I ask.

"I better start making a list and pick up groceries today," I mumble. "What's this meeting all about?"

Our family owned business is incorporated and we often have to hold a meeting to keep the board members happy. Before Cork retired he gifted all his stock to me and the boys.

"We think someone should be in the office to answer the phone and take messages all the time," Mike says. "It's becoming harder and harder for our customers to reach us. We also need someone to relay messages via the truck radios and be available to run supplies to us. We can save more time and miles."

"That's a good idea. Who do you have in mind for the job?" I ask.

"You," Cork answers. "Either you spend more time in the office or hire a girl and pay her out of your wages."

The telephone rings and it's my brother from Missouri.

"Mary went to the doctor this morning and I have to take her to Columbia, to the cancer hospital. The doctor's sure the lump is cancer. I don't know why she didn't tell me instead of waiting until it's too late. I'll get back to you when I know more. Will you go down and tell Mom and Dad?"

"Oh! no! Sure, I'll tell them. Do you need more money?"

"No, we're OK for now. Bye."

I turn from the phone, step on the puppy and burst into tears.

"Mary has cancer. After I tell my folks, I'll be in my bedroom praying. Please clear off the table and put your meeting on hold. Mike see if Veronica can help me with office duties." I run out the back door and jump in the car.

"I didn't know mom was religious. I've never seen her pray before," Jerry says.

"Neither have I," my husband answers.

Chapter Seven

HAVE FAITH

Reaching for the phone, I call my golf partner and postpone our match until later in the day. Then I spend an hour with Mom and Dad, assuring them that Mary's lump in her breast isn't going to be big enough to cause a problem.

"They can probably remove it and she'll be home in a few days," I tell them. "I've never spent much time praying and I know you haven't either, but I think this is a good time for us to start. May I say a prayer for Mary?"

"Please do," Mom says.

"Yes," echoes my Dad.

I start shaking like an alcoholic the morning after then I feel Jesus near and a calmness surrounds me. I am amazed at how easy the words tumble from my mouth.

"Dear Lord, you know I'm not good with words. We haven't talked much before and we don't spend a lot of time in church. You know Mary doesn't go to church at all. Maybe we don't have any right to come to you asking for help, but we don't know what else to do. We need you now more than ever before. If Mary's lump is cancer, we pray that you will heal her and touch her the way you are touching us here today."

I reach out and take hold of Mom and Dad's hands and continue my prayer. "Please watch over Dale and Mary as they travel to Columbia to the hospital. Give all of us the strength to get through this. I guess all we can do now is leave Mary in your hands and continue to pray that it's not too late for the doctors to help. Thank you. Amen."

Returning home I walk into the house to the sound of the clacking printer. Veronica calls out.

"Who is it?"

"Thanks for helping out. If the phone rings I'm not here, unless it's Dale," I say, as I walk into the bedroom and shut the door. My throbbing head reels. I feel like I've been run over by a truck and flop down on the bed. If I can only sleep for an hour I know I'll be refreshed and ready for the rest of the day. Whirling thoughts of Mary buzz through my mind.

The next thing I know it's three o'clock and I hear puppy sounds coming from under the bed.

"I can't believe Cork let you run loose in my house!" I squeal.

Sure enough the little piddler is under my bed and howling like a lost puppy. I grab her and carry her outside.

I walk around the house, puppy at my heels, to the garage and find the box she is supposed to be living in.

"Aren't you going to feed her?" Jesus asks.

I walk back through the basement and up the stairs to warm her milk. The phone rings twice.

"Take a message," I call out to Veronica, "I'm gone." I take the puppy back to the garage and put her in the box.

"I don't think you want to come with me to the golf course," I tell Jesus.

"I want to go with you everywhere."

"We have a match today with girls that curse if something goes wrong with their game," I answer.

"The girls are friends of mine," Beelzebub butts in. "There's nothing wrong with the way they talk."

I want to come, Jesus says. **"We'll figure out a way to handle the situation if it gets out of hand."**

When we arrive at the golf course Pat already has her cart out and our golf clubs loaded.

"I'm shaking like an old man. I don't know how I can play golf," my partner says, as we drive to the first tee. "I know you'll do all right, but Billie will stomp all over me. There isn't anybody I want to beat more. I hit a few practice balls. They went everywhere but where I aimed. Dear God, just don't let me make a fool of myself."

"My day hasn't been very good either," I tell Pat. "The good Lord knows we've had a bad day. If we do the best we can, and have faith, Jesus will help us. Let's take a deep breath, calm down and take one shot at a time."

"OK, but if I go all to pieces you remind me again," she answers.

I stay even with Janelle the first two holes. Pat is down two until the third hole when she chips in for a bird on the par three. We shout for joy and exchange high fives. Billie, her opponent, three putts and takes a double bogey. It evens up their match.

The air turns blue with profanity. "If you hadn't been shouting' I'd have made that putt," she said.

That's all Pat needed to boost her morale. The next hole has a big lake right in front of the green. Pat hits her second shot beautifully over the lake and onto the green. She looks at her club and says, "Oh, no! This club isn't mine where did it come from?"

"That's my club. How did it get in your bag?" Billie asks. "You hit my club. That's a two stroke penalty."

"I must have picked it up on the last hole. I'm sorry. I know it's a penalty," Pat said.

On the next hole my drive takes a sharp right turn and ends up in tall weeds.

"Nobody's looking. Set it up on something or kick it out into the short grass," Bub snarls. Without thinking I nudge my ball into shorter grass.

"What do the rules say about playing the ball as it lies?" Jesus asks.

"This is one of the new holes. We've been setting our ball up in the rough within six inches," I say looking sheepish.

"You have to beware of Bub every minute. He's lurking behind every blade of grass," Jesus says. **It was Bub that placed the wrong club in Pat's bag."**

"I don't think I'll ever be good enough to be a Christian. I'll declare a penalty on myself when we get to the green," I mumble. A sneaky smile creeps over my opponents face when she hears that I'm now two strokes down.

On number six I shank a shot into Barracuda Lake. "Oh shhhiit," I yell out for everyone to hear, slamming my club into the ground.

"That's another penalty," Bub chimes in.

"Hmmm, seems like your opponents aren't the only ones with unnecessary words," Jesus says.

"I've tried to get rid of that word, but it wants to slip out every time I do something dumb. This game is so frustrating it can make a preacher cuss!

It's Bub again. Here's something you can try that will help your game. Every time you do something good say, 'Praise The Lord!"

By this time I'm two strokes down and Pat is even. Approaching number 8 Pat's chip shot clunks in the hole again. She whoops and hollers. I give her a high five and say "Praise the Lord!" All eyes look at me funny and we proceed to the next hole.

My opponent three putts and mumbles unkind words under her breath. I sink a long putt clear across the green and even up the match again.

"Praise the Lord!" I shout.

"This games not turning out to suit me. I'm going to make the wind blow," Bub shouts, as the wind kicks up and my lucky hat cartwheels down the fairway faster than the ball.

I'm down one again and wishing the game was over. Billie and Janelle tee off first booming their drives down the middle of the fairway, 100 yards from the green.

I swing at the ball and watch it launch down the fairway with the wind behind it. My ball bounces past theirs about ten feet. "Praise the Lord," I shout.

"Curses," Bub mumbles.

The other two girls hit low running approach shots and the wind carries them zooming over the back of the green.

"Better use your putter," Janelle says, "or you'll be over there with us."

I feel quite confident in my approach shots because they are high soft ones. Taking out my pitching wedge I hit a high shot that bounces once on the green, hits the pin and falls in the hole for an eagle. I had a 2 on my scorecard.

"Praise the Lord," I shout into the wind, thinking they probably hear me back at the clubhouse. Pat and I hug, dance around and cry out with joy. My opponent takes a five and I'm two up.

After that Pat's opponent self-destructs. We don't hear anymore cussing. On the last hole Pat pulls her drive into a grove of trees.

"Oh, no! I can't get out of here! What am I going to do? Now I'm going to lose my match."

"Just keep your cool. Don't panic now. You have an opening straight out into the fairway. Keep your head down and hit the ball. I'll watch where it goes. We can do all things through Christ who strengthens us." Pat looks at me funny as we both wonder if I really said that.

She chips out into the fairway doing exactly what I tell her. We win the match with two strokes to spare. We are greeted in the club house with shouts of joy and congratulations. Our opponents head for the bar cursing and drowning their sorrows. Several girls offer to buy us drinks. I settle for ice tea, popcorn and a short time to bask in the afterglow of a triumphant win.

The quiet of a bright orange sunset and a peaceful breeze rustling the leaves settles me down from the clouds.

My thoughts return to Mary. I finish my tea and head for the car. Back to the chaos at home.

Chapter Eight

THERE'S STILL HOPE

Arriving home I find my husband watching TV with the hound dog in his lap.

"We won our match! We won! We won! Praise the Lord. We won our match! We won the tournament," I say, dancing around in circles. The puppy barks at me while I give Cork a blow by blow account of our successful round of golf.

"I don't believe it. How can all that happen in one match?" Cork asks.

Recognizing that I have an opening to tell Cork about Jesus, I approach it carefully. "We had inside help," I tell him. "I took Jesus with me today. I felt his presence by my side all afternoon. Jesus helped us win the game."

"Have you flipped your lid? What are you talking about?"

"Last Sunday, at church, I decided to take Jesus home with me. I'm making up my mind if I want to be a Christian."

I think you've been out in the sun and wind too long. Maybe you should quit playing so much golf. Your brain's getting fried.

"I do wish you'd listen. I want you to get to know Him too. I want us to attend church together and learn more about Jesus. I want to introduce you to Him."

"Don't listen to her! She's crazy!" Bub shouts.

"Not now, the dog and I are busy," Cork adds.

"Speaking of dogs. I thought this pup was going to be an outside dog. Our last puppy stayed in the garage until she learned where to make her messes. I've already cleaned up six puddles today. Please take her outside."

"She's too little. This is her first night away from her brothers and sisters. She'll freeze."

"Baloney! Dogs are supposed to have enough fur to keep them warm. If you let her run loose I'll throw both of you out in the garage. Please get a box and keep her in it."

I check the telephone answer machine to see if Dale called while I was out.

"Any messages from Dale?" I ask.

"Not while I was home," Cork answers.

"I'm going to the office and work on invoices right after I throw a load of clothes in the dryer. I'll bring the dog's box in from the garage and she can sleep in the basement," I tell him.

At 11pm I finish the invoices and write checks to pay more bills. While washing my face preparing for bed I hear Cork dragging the dog's box up the stairs.

"I thought we agreed the dog should stay in the box, in the basement," I holler at him.

"No, you agreed. The dog and I didn't have any say about it. I'm going to put her here by my side of the bed."

"Not in the bedroom. She stinks," I shout at him as I stick my head out of the bathroom door and step barefooted into a squishy pile of dog doo.

"It's Bub at work again," Jesus assures me as warm tears roll off my cheeks dropping silently onto the plush carpet. I hop on one foot back into the bathroom, run bath water, wipe off my foot and clean up the mess on the carpet.

My bath over and ready for bed, I find Cork with his hand hanging over the edge of the bed, into the box, keeping the puppy warm. They are both asleep. Definitely something to be thankful for.

I mutter a short prayer. "Lord please give me the patience to live through having a husband with another dog."

Since it's men's day at the golf course I use Thursday for completing tasks that are started earlier in the week. I plan to hang around the house waiting for Dale to call about Mary.

"Why aren't we playing golf today?" Bub wants to know. I'm beginning to like it out there. Remember you have a tournament this weekend. You better practice. There's no way you can repeat last night's performance."

47

"No, we're not playing golf today. If I get A chance I'll show you I can repeat last night's performance. Don't you know? I have Jesus on my side. But right now I need to clean house, finish the washing and ironing and run errands. I will also have the boys after school today."

"Good I like Mitchell. He's the ornery one. We can have lots of fun together," Bub adds.

The phone rings and it's Dale.

"Hello Bernita. It's worse than we thought. The doctor performed a biopsy this morning. It's cancer. They want to remove the whole breast. Mary is in a frenzy. I don't know what to do with her," Dale says.

"Oh, No! That poor girl has been through so much," I say, as tears fill my eyes and overflow. I feel Jesus near and hear him whisper.

"Ask to speak to her. Maybe we can help soothe her pain."

"B-b-but, I don't know what to say."

"I'll help. I know you can do it."

"Are you in Mary's room? Can I speak to her?" I ask. Dale hands Mary the phone and I can hear her sobbing.

"Oh, Bernita! What am I going to do? They want to take my whole breast," I'm going to run around lop-sided. I don't want them to cut it off."

"Mary please listen. I know this is terrible for you. Surgically removing the whole breast may mean the cancer can be contained. I want to pray with you. Maybe God can help us understand and lead us to the right decision. OK?"

"I'm not sure there is a God. It's been many years since I even thought about God. I'm nothing but a sinner. How can God help me now?"

"Let's try" I tell her. "Dear God. We come to you today with a heavy heart. We don't know what to do. Help Mary

49

and the doctors make the best decision. She's scared, and doesn't know what to do. She needs to know your presence. Show her how to reach out and clasp your hand and trust you. All we can do now is turn Mary over to you and let you touch her with your tender healing care. Bless the doctors who will be caring for her. All these things we ask in Jesus name. A-men"

"Mary, remember that Jesus loves you and I love you. I'll come to you whenever you feel you want me. You say the word and I'll be there."

"Let me think about it. I feel better now that you prayed for me. They want to give me radiation and chemo- therapy before the surgery. I'll be here for a while. I have to have a bone scan and who knows what other tests too."

"You have my 800 number call me anytime if you want to talk. Mom and Dad send their love. Remember I love you and Jesus does too."

After hanging up I'm in a dither. "Did the prayer even make any sense? Did I really say all that?" I ask Jesus.

"No it didn't. You know she's going to die. She won't last two months you better go to her now. I'll go with you," Bub says.

"Your prayer was very good. God doesn't care for flowery words. He only asks that you come to him and trust him," Jesus answers.

"You can kiss that girl good-bye. She's a goner, Bub adds.

I burst into tears again. Jesus folds me into his arms and I feel a calmness unlike anything I've ever felt before. It's almost like I'm floating on a cloud.

The rest of the morning is spent with laundry and house cleaning. Three times I pick the puppy up, tuck her under my arm and carry her outside, back to the box in the basement. She keeps escaping and crying until she finds me.

By noon I quietly sit down to gather my thoughts. What if Mary needs me to come now? My mother's going to want to go too. How can I leave during the busiest time of the year?

"You should get in the car right now and go. Your husband will survive without you for a week. He'll just let the pup run all over the house while he's gone. Your sister's going to die. Are you going to sit there until it happens. Let's go, or do something!" Bub shouts.

"You need to talk to your parents again. They are waiting to hear from you. They need to be consoled. Why don't we visit with them then go visit your Aunt in the Manor and the friend in the hospital who's dying. If you keep busy doing things for others you won't have time to sit and worry. Don't listen to Bub. You can't give up hope. How about it?" Jesus asks.

"I'd like that," I answer. I was supposed to visit two weeks ago, but didn't have time. When people are sick and dying I don't know what to say."

After spending time with Mom, Dad and Carol, Jesus and I stop at the hospital to visit a man who is dying of cancer of the bone. Carl has been a friend of my family for many years. His wife sits by his side all day and night, afraid to leave him.

Carl's bed is rolled partly into a sitting position. A huge smile creeps across his face when he recognizes me. I reach to take his work-hardened hands into mine and he cries out in pain.

"I'm so sorry. I didn't know," I said. "My hands are cold, I wanted you to warm them for me."

51

"You reach out and take my hands gently and I will warm yours," Carl said. "My bones hurt so bad that I can't move without crying in pain. I have a broken arm from the nurses trying to move me. I know my time is near."

"You know Carl, I think Jesus is telling you to reach out and take His hand, so He can warm you and lead you to your new home, where there is no pain, no tears, only love. If you can trust Him you will find joy and peace forever. Can I pray for you?"

"Yes please do."

Chapter Nine

JESUS LOVES ME

Jesus and I make several stops visiting a short time with older members of the church who are alone and shut-in. When school is out we pick up Mitchell and Preston and spend time playing ball in the yard.

Jerry arrives to take the boys home. After they leave a quiet, like none I have ever experienced, settles over my life.

"There's something wrong," I tell Jesus. "All of a sudden I feel funny. Is Bub causing trouble again?"

"No, he's napping. You may feel good about what you've accomplished today. Often it's therapeutic to visit with others, sharing your faith and a small part of

yourself. Even though Mary is in a critical situation you can feel satisfied that you shared a prayer with her and left her in my Father's care. She also knows you will come when she needs you."

A howling coyote sound fills the air. When I find the yowling puppy she's lost in the unmowed grass with her little head high in the air howling. Picking her up, I tuck her under my arm and walk into the house.

Friday morning I rise with the same quiet peaceful feeling I experienced the night before. It's hard to understand where the feeling is coming from. I chase the puppy out from under the bed and clean up three puddles.

"Isn't it warm enough this animal could live outside now?" I ask my husband.

"No. She really likes it in here. Look at her she wants to be your friend."

"I have enough friends. I don't need her."

"Suit yourself, but she's staying. What are you going to name your new friend?"

"She's your dog you name her."

"Preston thinks we should call her Peaches."

"She's more like a Sassy. Every time I get after her she sasses me back. I'm going to call her Sassy."

Are we going to play in the couples golf league at five this evening?" my husband asks.

"Only if you put up a fence so we can leave this dog outside when we're gone. The whole house is starting to smell like a dog pound.

"OK, OK, I'll build a fence. See you tonight dear."

I start planning my schedule for the day, thinking this can be a day when I catch up on laundry, vacuuming and office work. The phone rings and my plans are put on hold.

"Hi Mom, it's Mike. Veronica has been having pains most of the night. I took her to the hospital, but the doctor says the baby's not ready yet so he sent her home. We're drilling a well two miles north of town. Will you check on her and stay close to the phone if she needs you? Come and get me if her labor pains increase. When the rigs running I can't hear the radio or cell phone."

"Sure Mike, I'll be glad to check on her. Have you called her mother to come yet?"

"No, she doesn't want to come too early so she can stay two weeks after the baby comes."

I hang up the phone and gather laundry and toys and head to the basement to fold clothes and iron. Half way down the stairs the phone rings again.

"Hi Mom, can you keep Preston today? The babysitter's kids have chicken pox," Jerry says.

"Sure. Why not? He can help me chase the puppy."

"I'm expecting a big delivery from Robert's Pump House. You'll have to open the shop for the driver. We also have another load of washed pea gravel coming about 10 o'clock. Can you be here when the truck arrives? We're drilling today. I'll drop Pres off in a few minutes."

"I'll do my best. We're having a baby today too. Don't hesitate to call me if there's anything else I can do."

"Thanks Mom, you're a jewel."

I feel dizzy and A searing pain starts at the back of my neck and works all the way to the top of my head.

"I think you should call Carol and your parents to see if there's anything you can do for them today too," Bub suggests.

Downstairs again I fold a load of clothes and unplug the iron. Jerry dumps Preston off and thanks me again for being there when he needs me. Preston and I start looking for the puppy and the phone rings again.

"Bernita," I hear Carol whisper into the phone. "I'm having hard chest pains. I called the doctor. It'll save me an ambulance fee if you can take me to the hospital right now."

"Hold on. I'll be right there."

Forgetting the puppy I gather up Preston and drive the four blocks to Carol's apartment. We grab her oxygen and help her into the car. Arriving at the hospital I leave Preston sitting in the waiting room reading a book and follow the nurse wheeling Carol to the emergency room.

"Looks like this may be the big one," the nurse says.

Many times before I've spent half the night sitting in the waiting room while Carol has chest pains. Most of the time I end up taking her home the next morning with a new batch of nitroglycerine pills. Carol is 49 years old. She had by-pass surgery three years ago. Now all the arteries are plugged again. The heart specialist says there isn't anything else he can do. Years of uncontrolled diabetes and smoking has caused the problem.

I glance up in time to see Preston come running down the hall with the book under his arm.

"Will you read to me gramma?" he asks. "Can I see the babies?"

While the nurses and doctor work on Carol, Preston and I walk to the nursery to see the babies. Then we proceed to the waiting room to read the book.

"Here's a book of Bible Stories. I want you to read to me about Jesus," Preston says.

"OK Preston. It says here that we're all God's children and we're one big happy family? Red, yellow, black or white all are precious in his sight."

"Let's sing Jesus Loves Me, gramma."

"Sure, you start, I'll join in."

"Jesus loves me this I know, for the Bible tells me so."

Both of us sing along and the soothing peace that enveloped me earlier in the day settles over me again. I feel Jesus near as I breathe deeply and allow the over-whelming despair to flow from my body. My headache goes away and we spend the next hour reading Bible stories and taking a short nap.

Finally the nurse arrives to say Carol is experiencing a heart attack. She will be in the heart unit until her condition improves. I may want to inform other members of the family. The doctor isn't sure how serious the attack is. Carol is sleeping now and can't see anyone for at least two hours.

Preston and I head for the shop where we check out messages on the answer machine. The gravel truck arrives and we tell him where to dump and leave a note on the door with my cell phone number for the supply truck driver. Then we drive across town to check on Veronica.

"I don't want to stop here gramma," Preston says. "Let's go to your house and bake cookies."

"We can't right now. We have to see if Veronica is ready to have her baby. Bring your trucks you can play with them in her house," I tell him, as I help him out of the seat belt and give him a hug. "You're a good boy today."

"I know," Preston answers. "Mommy said I was."

Veronica greets us with the news that her pains have almost stopped. I talk her into keeping Preston while I go pick up Mom and Dad and return to the hospital. I remind her of my cell phone number and leave her to play trucks with Preston.

I visit with Mom and Dad about Carol and make three phone calls to my brothers. Dale assures us that Mary is doing fine and he has everything under control there. Dad decides to stay at home and answer the phone while Mom and I return to the hospital. Our church is in the process of calling a new pastor and the interim is only here on Sundays. I begin to wonder what I will do. At the present I can't think of anyone to call.

When we arrive at the hospital Carol is awake and feeling better. The nurse assures us that her condition is stable, but another attack could follow. If we want to talk to the doctor he makes rounds at five o'clock.

"Why don't you pray with Carol and your Mother," Jesus suggests.

"How do I talk to her about dying? We've known for three years this could happen. It seems easier not to talk about it. Why don't we ever have a pastor when I need one? She needs someone who can ask her if she's made her peace with God and talk to her about you. How do I bring up the subject? My headache is coming back."

Don't panic. I'm right here. I know you can do it. You prayed with Mary yesterday. Don't worry about what to say. I'll help you," Jesus answers.

With Jesus hand on my shoulder I feel more confident and attempt to bring up the subject.

"Carol, do you believe in life after death?" I ask.

"I don't know," she answers. "If I have any more of these pains I'm going to be ready to find out."

"Maybe Bernita will pray for you," my mother says.

"I've been a sinner all my life, I doubt if God will even hear if you pray for me," Carol adds."

"It's never too late to confess your sins and accept Jesus as your Savior," I tell her.

58

"If you think there's hope for me you can pray," Carol says. Mom and I stand close to the bed and take Carol's hands into ours.

"Dear God in heaven, as Carol says, she is a sinner, but if she truly wants to be forgiven I pray that she will later speak to you alone and confess her sins. Lift her into your arms and help her feel comforted. Show her the narrow path where you want all of us to walk. Renew Carol's hope and when her time comes may she depart this life knowing Jesus loves her, knowing she has been forgiven and knowing you will accept her into your Kingdom."

"Oh, yes, Jesus, please forgive me," Carol adds.

"We want to pray now for Mary too," I continue, after a brief pause. "Please let her surgery be successful and help her to heal quickly. And Father, God, give Mom and Dad, and all of us, the strength to carry on when our burden seems too heavy to bear. In Jesus precious name we pray. A-men.

I take time to call Veronica and see how she is progressing. Preston is taking a nap and her pains have come back, but they are light and every fifteen minutes. Mom and I hang around the waiting room until my cell phone signals it's time to return to the shop to unload a truck. I take Mom home so she can update Dad and I help unload freight at the shop. Then I drive to the well sight where the guys are drilling.

After bringing everyone up to date on the days happenings I return to Veronica's to pick up Preston and see how she is doing.

"I've given up on having a baby. It's never going to come. I'm calling my mother and get her on the way. She might as well be here for all the fun," Veronica says.

Preston and I pick up Mitchell at school and arrive home in time to fix supper for the hungry men in our life.

After informing Cork we weren't playing golf this evening I return to the hospital taking Carol a tape player with hymns and gospel music. This time she isn't interested in watching TV. I find her sitting and staring off into space.

"For some reason I feel calm and peaceful" Carol says. "My pain is gone and I seem surrounded by a marvelous glow."

"You've found Jesus, Carol," I tell her. "He loves you and has forgiven you. You can rest now knowing you have a home in heaven. Praise God."

Taking Carol in my arms we both cry tears of sadness because her time is drawing near and tears of joy because she feels the total and complete peace that comes from knowing Jesus.

Chapter Ten

COME WALK WITH ME

Saturday is our Annual Women's Open Golf Tournament with 60 ladies coming from area towns. I've been involved in the preparations and always look forward to the big day. My secret desire is to win this event at least once before I get too old to play. With all the excitement of Friday still in my mind, I feel a short moment of guilt about playing in the tournament.

"I want you to walk with me today," Jesus announces.

"You know I can't go today. I'm playing in a tournament," I tell him.

"It's decision time. Your week is almost up. I want you to follow me," he says.

"Don't listen to him," Bub chimes in. "He's always trying to spoil our fun. Why does he wait until the most important time in your life to want you to walk with him?"

"I can't do anything with you two arguing. I have to check on Carol and Veronica first," I tell them.

After calling the hospital I find that Carol has had a restful night but she remains in the Heart Unit. The nurse suggests I call the Doctor or be there at 8am when he makes rounds. When I talk to Mike about Veronica's condition I learn that her pains have stopped and her Mother is on the way.

"Let me take care of your family. Everything is under control. I need you to follow me today," Jesus repeats. **"Whoever desires to follow me will deny their own wishes, take up their cross and follow me."**

"B-buut, what about my family. I have two sisters in critical condition, a new grandchild on the way and two little boys who need someone to look after them. I haven't finished the office work, my house is dirty and my parents need me. How long will this walk take?"

"I can't tell you how long the walk will be. I hope we can always walk together. If you love your family more than me, you aren't worthy of my love," he answers.

"How disgusting! You can't seriously be contemplating doing what he asks," says Bub. "Don't worry about your family. What about the golf tournament? With my help you can win today. Let's go! It's only 30 minutes until tee time. You should be ashamed to be seen with him. He's crazy."

Jesus replies, **"Anyone who is ashamed of me and my words in this sinful generation, I will be ashamed of them when I come into the Glory of my Father. Get thee**

behind me Satan. I'm leaving in five minutes all who wish to follow may come."

"I do want to come with you Jesus. Please wait I'm not even dressed" I answer. "Should I fix something to eat? I haven't had any breakfast. What should I wear? How long will we be gone?" Should I bring my purse?"

"Curses!" shouts Bub and stomps off towards the golf course.

"Don't worry, saying 'what shall we eat or what shall we wear?" says Jesus. **"I know you need all these things. Seek My Father's Kingdom and everything else shall be given to you."**

"I don't know why you want me with all my problems. I'm guilty of wanting to play golf instead of taking care of my family. I'm a sinner. There's so much going on in my life. When I get up in the morning I don't know where to start. Can you help me?"

I make a grab for yesterday's clothes lying in a heap on the floor, slip on my sandals and run out the door.

"Wait Lord! I want to follow you. "Is it OK if I call you Lord?"

"Yes, I want to be your Lord and Master."

"Where are we going anyhow? I don't have on my walking shoes."

"You won't need purse or sandals where we are going. Your feet won't hurt as long as you follow me."

"But what about my back and legs? If I go very far without my walking shoes my back kills me."

"Trust me," He says, as we walk out of the yard and up the winding, uphill, dusty road that borders the East edge of our small town.

As we walk along the wildflowers burst into bloom and the Meadowlark's song fills the air. A frisky colt leaves his mother and bounds in our direction. It's as if the world comes to life the minute Jesus steps outside.

Chapter Eleven

"LOVE" THE GREATEST GIFT

All of a sudden the air is filled with yapping puppy cries again. Looking around I see Sassy bounding after me, almost lost in the wild flowers and cactus of the green grassed pasture.

"Damn! Why doesn't Cork take care of that dog? You can't come Sassy! I'll have to take her back. Will you wait for me, Jesus?"

"Let her come. Sassy loves you and she wants you to love her too. Pick her up and carry her. See how soft and fluffy she is. The most important lesson you can learn is how to Love. Are you afraid to show Love? Sassy will help you learn if you let her. She can't bear

being away from you. She's just a baby and misses her mother and needs to know that someone Loves her. See how she is licking your face. Feel the Love that flows from her small beating heart. Sassy has chosen you to Love unconditionally, as I have. Can you Love us as we Love you?"

"My family never expressed their Love. I know my parents loved me, but they never showed it. My husband grew up in the same atmosphere. We have trouble talking about our feelings. I'm afraid we have passed that trend on to our sons also. What can I do about it now?"

"Let the puppy be a reminder. She won't let you forget to Love her. You haven't given her a chance. Relax and look around you. Can't you see that your

husband needs someone to Love. He needs the puppy. He won't admit it, but he needs you to show your Love for him also. You can't share your Love for me until you learn to give Love freely to others.

"I'd like you to start reading the Bible. The New Testament is all about Love. If you Love first and have Faith in me I will walk with you and you with me. The World is full of trials and tribulations. Together there is no limit to what we can achieve. Without me you will continue to flounder like a fish out of water.

"In 1 Corinthians:13, NIV Paul teaches about Love. He says, (You can understand all mysteries, have knowledge, all faith, give all you have to feed the poor, but have not Love, and you have nothing. Love suffers long; does not behave rudely, is not provoked, thinks no evil, rejoices in the truth, and never fails. Abide faith, hope, Love, these three; but the greatest of these is Love.)

"There are so many commandments and laws. I don't know if I have time to read and learn all the rules. I know I'm a sinner. I don't take time to pray. I'm on the run all the time. Where do I start? Which is the greatest of all the commandments?"

Love the Lord your God with all your heart, soul and mind The second is like it. Love your neighbor as much as you do yourself. All of the law hangs on these two commandments.

"Do people really love their neighbor as themselves? Does that mean everybody? There are some people that are really hard to love."

"Let me teach you."

Setting Sassy on the ground I let her follow. She takes time to chase a butterfly and steps in a prickly cactus. Then

69

the yapping begins again. I pick her up and she licks my face as I remove the thorns. When the crying ceases she nuzzles up close to my neck and falls asleep.

"I may not show my Love, but I Love my family very much. How can I learn to Love you more than my family? My little grandsons are easy to Love. They give gramma hugs and are free with their kisses. Can I Love you more?"

"If you agree to follow me, I'll teach you everything you need to know. When you have learned the Love lesson we'll work on patience, trust and forgiveness. When you stumble I'll pick you up. When your burden is too heavy I'll carry you."

Chapter Twelve

TRUST, PATIENCE AND HARVEST

We continue walking over the grassy knolls and around the gullies washed deep from years of heavy rainstorms. A short distance away we can see farmers plowing under last year's wheat stubble. The odor of fresh turned earth permeates the air. Oil well pumping units stand tall on the horizon as the chug-chug of the engines signal the movement of black, heavy oil into the round, silver storage tanks.

"Sassy and I are thirsty. And hungry. We just walked right past the Burger King. There isn't anywhere else to get a breakfast biscuit and coffee if we keep going this way."

"You can't live on bread alone. I am the bread of life. Whoever comes with me will never be hungry, and whoever believes in me will never be thirsty. Those who hunger and thirst for God's approval will be satisfied.

Let's walk to the bottom of this hill where the creek runs under the bridge. We can drink from the creek and sit in the shade and rest," Jesus suggests.

I don't think it's safe to drink the water. There's cattle in the pasture all along Lodgepole Creek. Today everything's polluted."

The sound of clear, cool water rushing over the rocks draws us near. Placing Sassy on the ground I watch as she hurries towards the stream. She jumps in without a moments hesitation, drinks her fill, then walks in deeper and lets the cool water wash around her tummy.

This water is clear Bernita. Can you be like Sassy and trust me? Can you step in and drink your fill? Can you walk in the deepest part and trust that I won't let any harm come to you? Can you completely give your life to me, so that I can mould you into the person I want you to be?"

"I think I see now what you want me to do. You are trying to teach me by telling parables, like you taught the disciples many years ago, aren't you?"

I lower myself to the soft, green grass, cup my hands and drink deeply from the cool water. Then I take off my shoes and socks, wade in the creek and listen intently as Jesus continues teaching.

"Life isn't always easy. There will be rough times ahead. If you believe and have faith in me, no matter what happens, we can weather the storms together. I want you to take up your cross daily and follow me.

"This week has been a trial for you. We are embarking on a journey. I can't promise you the road will always be smooth. Some of your friends and family don't know me. Together we can plant the seed of my love within their hearts. But without water, sunshine and nourishment that seed will never grow. Someone needs to pray for them and offer guidance. When the time is right they will want to follow.

Bernita, do you understand the parable about the farmer who planted his seeds?"

"I've heard sermons about it, but most of the time I didn't pay any attention. I'm not a farmer so I didn't think it had anything to do with me. What does it mean?"

"The seed is God's Word. Some people are like seeds that were planted along the road. They hear the word, but then the devil comes. He takes the word away from them so they won't believe and become saved."

"I've felt that tension, Lord. Like someone pulling me away."

"Some are like seeds among the rocks. They welcome the word with joy when they hear it, but they don't develop good roots. Some believe for a while, but when their faith is tested, they bail out, blaming God for their problems. The seeds that were planted among thorns are people who hear the word, but the worries, riches and pleasures of life choke them. They don't produce anything good. The seeds that were planted on good ground are people who hear the word, but keep it in their hearts and produce what is good no matter what life may bring."

"If I understand you right, if your roots are imbedded deep enough in my heart, you will sustain me even though the devil is constantly intervening, tempting and pulling me in the other direction."

"Now you're getting the right idea."

"Oh! I see now. If I invite you into my heart you want me to feed and water the seeds you plant in the people around me. As the seeds grow you reap the harvest. Right?"

"Right on! You are picking this up quickly. Only sometimes I need you to plant the seed."

"I'm such a sinner. How can you not condemn me?"

"There is no condemnation with me.

"Here comes the devil now. He won't ever leave you alone. He is a persistent little devil, always luring my people into traps and bunkers. You can take the easy

way out and hitch a ride home with him, or we can continue our walk and talk together.

When I look around the largest dust devil I have ever seen is coming right at us.

"I'm not through talking yet. I have more questions that need answered. Let's duck into this old barn until he gets tired of blowing."

Creaking and groaning like an old man the barn continues to protect us through the dirt swirling storm. When a quiet calm settles over the countryside Jesus and I continue walking and talking.

"My family is a mixed bag when it comes to religion." I tell Him. "We have Lutherans, Presbyterians, Baptists and some aren't anything. I know people who believe that if you aren't a member of their church or denomination you won't be welcome in God's Kingdom. Is that true?"

"In my Kingdom there is but one church. It's not your place to judge other's faith. Let me be the judge. It's where your heart is that counts. If there's room in your heart for me, and you love me, we will live together in Paradise forever. You must choose whom you will follow."

"But it's not easy for me, Lord."

"I know it's not easy, Bernita. You are only human.

"The gathering of believers, the church, is very important. When you meet together you build and strengthen each others faith. My only hands, feet and voice in the world today is through my body of believers. What you do for the least of these brothers, friends, and neighbors of yours, you do for me. I don't care which church they belong to."

"What about the different Bibles.? Catholics, Mormons, Jehovah's Witness', King James, NIV, NKJV and ten or twelve other versions. It's confusing to me."

"Choose a translation of my Word and a church that teaches it in its truth and purity. Continue to study the Bible and your faith will grow. Don't try to change the meanings of the words you find there. I will speak to you through the Scriptures. Beware of false prophets."

"It's hard to know about false prophets. My husband says I'd fall for anything, including you. He thinks I would buy the Empire State Building for $50 if someone offered it to me. I don't think that would be a bad deal. I know a guy who bought the London Bridge and tore it down, shipped it to Arizona and rebuilt it. He's made a lot of money off of that bridge. The Empire State Building might look better here in small town America than it does in New York City."

"I'm talking more about people who claim to know everything about God's Kingdom and try to convince you that they have been sent by God to lead you into a cult or compound that is ruled by them. You may even find this kind of prophet in your local church. My Father is the only one who knows when I will be returning. Yes, I'm here for you this week because you chose to take me home with you. I am here waiting for all who seek me.

"I worry about how long it takes for your plan to work? I've been going to church for 50 years and, until now, never really knew you. Are there more people like me? Sometimes it takes too long for prayers to be answered. I don't have patience. I'm stubborn, greedy, envious and think sinful thoughts. Sometimes I cheat, lie and say bad words. Can you use someone like me? Can you love me when I'm like this?"

"**I know Bernita, but I love you unconditionally. We can work on one thing at a time. Let's start with patience.**"

"**One day with me is like a thousand years and a thousand years is like one day. I am not slow to do what I promise as some may think. I am patient for your sake. I want all people to have an opportunity to turn to me and change the way they think and act. Think of my patience as an opportunity for all to be saved.**"

"As I get to know you better, Lord I'm thankful you are patient. I know it will take me a long time to learn."

"**Can you see how I have been patient with you for fifty years? Your mother and Sunday School teachers started you on your faith journey when you were a small child. Look back over your life. Can you see that I have protected you and kept you from harm? I chose you a long time ago. I've been knocking on the door of your heart for years. It's getting late in your life. It's time to deepen your faith. I've had patience with you. Now trust me and learn patience.?**"

Chapter Thirteen

FORGIVENESS

Jesus and I rise together and begin to walk, following the tree-lined creek. We pass by grazing black and white spotted cattle with their tails briskly swatting at pesky flies. Sassy is enjoying the walk and comes nose to nose with a frisky young calf frolicking near the creek. The calf snorts and scares her. She comes running and I pick her up again. She cuddles in my arms and goes to sleep.

As we approach Ferguson's Grove hundreds of screeching black Starlings wake Sassy as they take flight from the naked, towering cottonwood trees. She squirms and kicks, wanting to be free. Setting her on the ground, I watch as she makes an attempt at chasing the noisy birds.

"How far are we walking today?" I ask.

"It's almost time for me to leave you. Before we end our walk I want you to be willing to follow me. There's one last thing I want to ask you. Have you forgiven everyone who has wronged you?"

"Well, m-most of the time I don't have any trouble forgiving others.

"Do you hold grudges against your neighbors?"

"No, I get along fine with my neighbors. They don't bother me and I don't bother them."

"Have you learned to turn the other cheek? Do you feel you have to get even when somebody wrongs you? Do you love your enemies and bless those who curse you?"

"Turning the other cheek isn't easy. I'm not a fighter, but I am a coward. I walk away from adversity. Do you have room in your Kingdom for cowards? I've never thought about blessing someone who curses me. That's a good idea. A person would feel bad after curseing you if you blessed him."

"The object isn't to make others feel bad or to get even. It's more important that you understand the value of doing good. Whoever asks you to go one mile, do you go with him two?"

"Yeah, I try to go an extra mile with people. There have been times that I've turned down requests for money. Seems like everybody wants a hand out. How do we know who really needs it?"

"Give to the mission projects your church supports and local charities. The world is full of crooks and thieves. Pray about it. Together we'll decide who is worthy. How about doing good to those who hate you and praying for those who are spiteful and persecute

you? Your church has had trouble keeping a pastor. Pastors aren't perfect any more than you are. Have you forgiven and prayed for the pastors who are gone?"

"Once when I was a kid I lied and got my brother in trouble. That lie sure got heavy carrying it around for 50 years. Last year I asked him to forgive me and he did. That was a big relief."

"But what about forgiving those who have wronged you? If we are to continue our walk, your slate needs to be wiped clean. I can wash your sins away, but you must first be reconciled to your brother, son, daughter, friend, neighbor or enemy. If you are unwilling to forgive others do you think it's fair for me to forgive you?"

"I was on the board when one of our Pastors was released. I was hurt and angry. Maybe I haven't completely forgiven him. How can I turn loose of the hurt? Is it necessary to keep forgiving over and over again?"

"Yes, Bernita. That is my way. Can you learn to love people like that? Love them as much as I love you. Hate the sin but love the sinner. Remember I am the judge. Your job is to love and forgive. Lose the extra baggage. Your burden will be lighter. Then you can follow me."

"I'll need help. Can you help me love others as much as you love me?"

"Now you have the right idea. Ask and you will receive. Search and you will find. Sometimes the answer may be No. Your newly learned patience and trust will carry you through the waiting. Think what my world will be like if everyone practices love, trust, patience and forgiveness."

"What a bright, warm, peaceful, loving world this will be," I answer. "You said you were leaving. Where are you going?"

"Tomorrow is Sunday. You agreed to take me home for just a week, remember? Although we have walked and talked together and you have felt my presence with you. The sense of peace you feel is the Holy Spirit. It's time for me to move on. I am returning to my Father. I will not leave you without a Helper. We can continue our walk until it's time for your journey home. If you follow me, do all that I have taught you, our walk together will be fruitful."

"I don't understand the Spirit, and what does it mean to be born again?"

"Come, I'll teach you."

Chapter Fourteen

THE HOLY SPIRIT

We continue walking along the creek as it winds it's way through pastures, busy farmyards and nearby cornfields. The spicy aroma of blossoming lilac bushes and the bright fuscia blooms of a flowering crab waft across our path as we pass through a farmer's yard. The clickity-clack of a whirring windmill as it turns into a light southwest wind greets us as we continue our westward journey. The steady hum of truck traffic along Interstate 80 to the south and the shrill whistle of a freight train traveling the Union Pacific Railroad to the north signal the fact that life goes on, even though I have taken a day off. Sassy runs into a cornfield, with plants high enough to hide her, stopping long enough to lap up irrigation water trickling slowly down the long straight rows. "Sassy, come back," I holler. "You'll get lost in there."

"She'll be OK," Jesus says. **"She can't get lost while following me and neither can you. You will never be alone, because I will be with you always.**

"But, you said you have to leave. I don't understand.

"If you love me and want to walk with me you will keep my commandments. I will ask my Father and He will send you a helper to be with you always. You won't be able to see Him but you will know Him, because the Spirit will be in you. My helper, The Holy Spirit, the Spirit of God, will teach you everything and remind you of all I have told you. The Spirit is recognized only by those who have learned to love one another as I have loved you."

"I must really be dense. I hear you but it's not registering."

"We still have a long walk. Soon I will reveal the Spirit to you. Come let's walk faster. Sassy is tired. Her little legs aren't as long as ours."

"I'm getting tired too!" I say, as I stoop to pick her up. She yelps holding one paw in the air. Checking her foot I discover a clump of cockle burrs in her front paw and stuck to the long hair of her furry legs and chest."

"Look at the mess you're in. If you'd stay close to me this wouldn't happen," I tell her.

"Now you're getting the idea. No matter where you go there will always be thorns. Sassy is like you, she wanders away. She's nosy and wants to inspect everything. She doesn't completely trust you. You can teach her to trust you and stay close like I am teaching you."

"I know I ask silly questions, and I have felt your presence this week, but I don't understand how this helper of yours plans to assist me with family problems. What can He do? One of my sisters is dying, the doctors can't do anything more for her, another has breast cancer. I should be with her! We've prayed, but I can't see that it's doing any good! My parents are aging and need me. I have grandsons I want to spend time with, a family business to help run, and my husband brings me home a new puppy. They are all interfering with my golf game! And on this busy day I left it all to follow you. What if Veronica is having her baby now? I'm getting anxious and my headache is coming back."

"It's your choice. I can't promise that life will be fair only that I will be there in the form of the Holy Spirit, a comforter to lean on and help make decisions. Like Sassy, you will have thorns cropping up in your life. You don't have to be everything to everybody. That's my job. But you are my hands and feet. I need you to tell people about your walk with me. I want you to be equipped and ready for your family and friends when they need you. Sometimes you don't have to say anything. Just be there. Let those around you see me through your actions and deeds. Plant a seed wherever you can. I'll reap the harvest."

"But how can I do it all?"

"You need help to sort out your priorities. What is most important in your life right now?"

"G-g-olf—and my family. My little grandsons are the most precious of all."

"Is it necessary to play golf every day? Can you set aside two or three days a week to help your family and

be about my Father's business as well as the family business?"

"It takes only half a day to play golf, unless I play an out of town tournament, which sometimes takes three whole days. Most weeks I have at least six half-days for all my other activities. Unless—we stay and play more golf. Or sit around and talk about the shots we missed. I don't play on Thursday. That's mens day. If I had more time for me I'd write a book. Maybe I could hire someone to clean my house."

"Sounds like the Spirit is going to have a full time job re-adjusting your attitude. Then your priorities. But that's the Spirit's job."

"Let's walk to the south around the face of the dam. It will be quieter there. We can find a shade tree and a log to rest on. All along the creek and the lake, hundreds of cottonwood trees died a few years back when the dam was drained," I tell Jesus. "It used to be for irrigation but now it's a recreation area for boaters, fishermen, swimmers and a refuge for birds. Many new trees have been planted and watered by Bill Batterton over the years. Is he one of your helpers."?

"Yes, I know Bill, the local tree man. It takes all kinds of people to be about my Father's business. He is a steward of the land. Come, let's go near the water here and rest."

I find a comfortable log with a back rest. Sassy slides from my lap and goes to the water. It's quite peaceful sitting there as the light feathery clouds drift across the azure-blue sky. The far off cry of a gull and a speeding motorboat break the silence. I slip back into the peace that surrounds me and fall fast asleep. Sassy wakes me as she yips at a bark colored toad and a snapping turtle. The turtle draws into her shell. Sassy grabs the toad in her mouth and carries it to me. Suddenly she spits it out, shaking her head and runs back to the water to splash and drink.

"Even the lowly toad has a way of defending itself," **Jesus says. "The bitter taste left by the toad will keep** **Sassy from grabbing it again. You don't realize it but** **you are a little like Sassy, and a little like the turtle.** **Like Sassy, you want to help everyone, yet you spend** **the majority of your time playing golf. You can't do it** **all. Like the turtle you are timid and withdraw into** **your shell keeping me at a distance. You are hiding the** **talent God gave you. When you are ready, the peace** **that passes all understanding can be yours today."**

"I really am tired, frustrated, worn out and helpless. I know I can't do anything by myself. I've tried and it isn't working. Yes, Lord, I need a helper. I'm ready to completely follow you. Earlier as I sat on the log and fell asleep a peace flowed over me like a ray of sunshine on a cold windy day."

"While you were sleeping I prayed for you. Come **down near the water. It is time for me to leave. You** **were baptised with water, in the name of the Father,** **Son and Holy Spirit when you were twelve years old.** **But you haven't really accepted the gift that I offer.** **Don't you see that Father, Son and Holy Spirit are one?** **God is Spirit. When your pastor talks about the Trinity** **he is talking about God, who came to earth as the Son,** **Jesus. When Jesus left on the day of Pentecost, to sit at** **the right hand of God the Father, He promised to** **return. Until then He left the Holy Spirit to teach, lead** **and guide you. I am here to make sure you understand** **as you are baptized with the Spirit. The Spirit in you is**

the only way God's Church and His Kingdom can grow."

"How will I know this Spirit?"

"Many times this week you have talked about a peace coming over you. You will feel your burdens lifted and a true sense of peace in your heart. The Kingdom of God starts right here—right now, the minute you accept my offer. Don't you see? The Kingdom of God is within you."

A bright glow surrounds Jesus while a white dove flies down from the rustling branches of the cottonwood tree and lands on Jesus' shoulder. I fall to my knees folding my hands in prayer while watching His face. The dove flies to my shoulder as a warm glow fills my heart. With eyes closed I thank God for His precious gift. When I open my eyes Jesus is gone.

Chapter Fifteen

I DECIDE TO FOLLOW JESUS

When I wake from what seems to be a pleasant dream, Jesus is gone. I stay in a kneeling position for twenty minutes basking in the afterglow of Jesus' presence. The lake slaps at the shoreline, leaves still rustle in the cottonwood trees, but a stillness like none I have ever experienced surrounds me. The toad, turtle and Sassy sit side by side staring at me as an overwhelming fishy odor brings me back to reality.

"Sassy! You didn't find a dead fish to roll in did you? Look at you! You have to learn to be a little lady. Are you happy with your new perfume?"

My knees creak as I try to rise from my kneeling position and my hips and back ache from walking further than I've ever walked before.

"Welcome back to reality," I mumble to myself. "Guess the devil has caught up with us again." Then I realize we are ten miles from home and I don't have my cell phone. I carry Sassy to the water and do my best to wash the smelly dead fish off the squirming little mutt. She shakes herself and most of the cold fishy water lands on me.

We walk back along the face of the dam towards Highway 30, which runs along the dams north side. Perhaps we can flag down a motorist and catch a ride back to town. At the moment I can't imagine who will stop for a wet, fishy hound dog and a windblown, gray haired grandma. Then I remember the gift Jesus left with me. We reach the highway and my heart swells with joy as I gaze in wonder at this beautiful world God has created. I breathe deeply taking in the fresh country air. Sheep graze near the road and Sassy runs into the ditch, chasing them away from the fence.

"Don't chase the sheep away, Sassy. Jesus is the Shepherd, we are the sheep. Stay close and follow me," I tell her.

We take off at a faster pace as I jog a while, then skip like a young school girl, forgetting my pain. I start singing, "I have decided to follow Jesus, I have decided to follow Jesus. No turning back. No turning back."

Maybe being older is just a state of mind, I think to myself. If I just didn't have to look in the mirror. I feel light as a feather skipping along as we pass the weathered fence posts and remains of the old irrigation flumes that used to carry irrigation water over the ravines. The pasture land is full of the spikey planted, pale yellow blooming yucca.

Black and all white cattle stand in mixed groups around the creek, chewing their cuds. It reminds me of how much Jesus loves everyone and no matter our color we must all stand together. Ahead of us a chicken hawk dives to the ground, plucking a little gray mouse from the field. A pair of large crows caw loudly at a redwinged black bird. No cars pass. There is no one to give us a ride.

Sassy is dry and I carry her a while. She snuggles into a comfy position and falls asleep. We stop again for a rest and drink of water in Ferguson's Grove along Lodgepole Creek.

"It seems like nobody else is in the world today." I tell Sassy. We walk back to the highway and I begin skipping again, turning around in circles and holding Sassy high in the air. "I think we've been **born again**," I tell her. Then I sing again. "There's Joy, Joy, Joy, Joy, down in my heart. Down in my heart to stay". We are almost home. Who cares if we get a ride. Maybe the guys will still be at the shop and can take us the rest of the way home. Then I hear a truck slow down behind us.

"What in the h—are you doing out here dancing on the highway?" My son Jerry hollers out the window.

"Did your car break down? We didn't see it along the road," my husband chimes in. "I thought you were golfing today."

"No, not today," I answer. "We decided to follow Jesus."

Chapter Sixteen

A LICENSE TO CARE

"Now we have a license to care," I said as we walked out of church together after receiving our certificate for finishing the Covenant For Caring program.

My friend Doris turned to me and asked, "Why did we have to wait for this certificate before showing care and concern for others in our church and community?"

I thought for a minute, then I knew. I had been too busy worrying about myself and my problems to notice other people's needs. Now the Holy Spirit was moving in my life and was arousing in me a desire to help others. I was feeling ready now to be one of God's assistants.

After a week of taking Jesus with me, I seemed drawn to stop at the church office. I had never been in the pastor's office and felt uncomfortable. I wasn't the type of person to get involved with programs and studies. What in the world would I do if somebody called on me to say a prayer or asked a question about the Bible? By the time I find a Bible verse the reading is over. Since the Spirit was alive and working in my life, I was filled with enthusiasm and wanted to be involved in the life of the church, but I still had personal problems. After a brief greeting I shared my own concerns.

"My family seems to be falling apart and I need guidance." Tears flowed while I continued telling the pastor my story. I was upset last year when a granddaughter was stillborn and nobody from the church called on me. One of the reasons I belong to a church is to have support when things go wrong. I've always thought the church is supposed to be available for baptizing, marrying and burying. Now I have a son going through a divorce, elderly parents to care for and family members who are dying," I told the pastor. "I don't know how to care for others who are hurting, and losing a daughter-in-law is like having a death in the family," I sobbed.

The pastor rose from his chair, gently touched my shoulder as he reached to close the door. Settling back in his chair he started asking probing questions that seemed to bring out the frustration and pain. He offered counsel using scripture that was fitting and healing to my situation. He invited me to meet with him whenever I felt tension building. He suggested I might find the Covenant For Caring program helpful. It was to begin the next Sunday evening. Then he prayed with me. I cried throughout the prayer but left the church feeling calm and an unbelievable peace, like Christ was there with His healing touch. I felt assured that once again I must let the Lord take charge.

It was difficult deciding if I really wanted to attend the Covenant For Caring class. Didn't I have my hours filled to the maximum already? By evening each day I am bushed. All during the week I felt the pull of the Spirit. and finally gave in. I told myself if I were uncomfortable attending I wouldn't go again.

The goal of the caring program was to create caring people out of everyday people like me. Teaching us how to care for others and share our faith. Sharing and caring working together as a team helps us to spread God's word to others.

Our class started with 12 persons. When we met the first night, we were all mumbling and grumbling. We had no desire to be evangelists.

"Let's leave the evangelizing to Billy Graham and the other TV preachers. Just show us what we can do here in our little church to make it come to life and grow," one of the men said.

Each of us came to the first meeting for various reasons. Frances felt there should be more visiting with the elderly and shut-ins. After all, the pastor didn't have the time to make all the visits necessary. One couple had an elderly father living with them. They needed support. I had three people in my family who were dying of cancer or heart disease.

The caring program was a taped presentation. All we needed was a VCR and a TV set and simple instructions the ordinary layperson could easily follow and understand. Our pastor served as the leader. Narrators gave instructions, then there was a short break while we carried them out.

We split into groups of four and were asked to share our faith with one another. One talked while the others practiced active listening. Right away my heart sank because I didn't know what I was going to share. Then I thought about my experience of welcoming the Holy Spirit into my heart. Surely my fellow church members would believe me.

The story flowed from the depths of my being. Nobody thought I was crazy or looked at me like I was from outer space. What a joy to know there were others whose heart was full of the Spirit and understood and shared my feelings. I knew I would attend the rest of the meetings.

We drew names and each of us was instructed to show special caring for that person during the week. We were to perform this without letting him/her know who was doing the caring. There were caring gifts showing up everywhere that week: a plate of homemade cookies left in a car after church on Sunday; a happy face painted on a pumpkin, deposited on a doorstep on Halloween; special prayers on Sunday morning for our loved ones, notes, phone calls and offers of help after an injury.

We had so much fun we could actually see how comforting these small things were and so we drew names again the next week. "It's easy to show caring for someone when it's an assignment," Bill said. "It gives you a wonderful feeling, knowing that small caring gifts can make a shut-in's day or boost their moral. Why haven't we been doing this all the time?"

In class we split into teams of two and practiced calling on two others. Through role-playing we discovered real talent in our group and became more comfortable with the procedure.

When the class was completed we were called to the front of the church one Sunday morning during worship service to receive our certificates and take our vows of commitment.

We agreed to the following group covenant:

1. To pray regularly for the persons on our caring list.
2. To seek opportunities to grow in relationship to God through Bible Study and Prayer..
3. To take responsibility for listening and caring for one other person at all times.
4. To be actively involved in the life of the church.
5. To care and support other members of the community.
6. To maintain confidentiality at all times.

I discovered evangelism isn't just knocking on doors and preaching. The church's main goal doesn't have to be growing in numbers. I grew in faith and love for Jesus Christ as we studied. The program proved to me that evangelism can work even within oneself as well as within a church community, bringing people closer to our Lord every day through Christ like caring.

A new interim pastor arrived at our church shortly after the conclusion of our training. His stay would only be for one year. Rev. James requested that one member from our group accompany him to assist him in getting acquainted with church members.

When my turn arrived I wasn't sure what to expect. As we drove to Mrs. Keller's house I kept looking around to be sure nobody saw me riding around town with the preacher. What would people in a small town think?

Mrs. Keller's husband had just passed away and she was experiencing profound grief. We visited for a while, but mostly just listened and encouraged her to share her feelings as she related the last moments with her husband. Then we held hands and prayed together. Afterwards she cried and hugged me, thanking me for coming. It was one of the most touching experiences of my life. I knew I'd be back to visit her soon and often.

"It means a lot to have a representative from the congregation along on calls. People get the idea someone besides just the pastor cares for them," Rev. James said.

The Rev. John Warning, retired after 50 years in the ministry, visited our church one day to fill the pulpit. His sermon was a reflection of his ministry. He said, "If there were one thing I could do over, it would be to spend more time in prayer and teaching Bible study. I'd leave more of the caring to the congregation."

Caring became a part of my life. From that point on I often found my spiritual batteries re-charged each time I reached out in love and caring to another of God's children.

I found, as so often is true, that there was a reason I didn't receive a call from the church when our granddaughter was stillborn. I hadn't called anyone to report our loss or to ask for prayers.

No longer am I timid about asking for help. As a member of God's caring community, I know now that I am called to minister to others as well as asking others to minister to me.

Chapter Seventeen

GOD'S GENTLE REMINDERS

Now that I was equipped with the many lessons a Christian needs to survive in life—love, trust, patience, forgiveness, joy and caring, along with the gift of the Holy Spirit,—how was that knowledge going to affect my life? With all of this I still wasn't certain that I knew enough. I started listening to the sermons and discovered that most of the time our preacher knew what he was talking about. Even the words to hymns took on a new meaning.

I attended a Bible Study because I had a deep desire to learn more. I still had questions. I felt uncomfortable because I didn't know the Bible well enough to find the verses right away. The leader was patient and didn't look at me like I was crazy when I asked dumb questions.

I noticed verses from the Bible actually applied to me.

"Take up the whole armor of God so you can stand against the wiles of the devil," Paul says in his letter to the Ephesians Chpt-6:11-15 NKJ. *"Shod your feet with the preparation of the gospel of peace, above all take the shield of faith so you will be able to quench all the fiery darts of the devil.*

"Isn't it amazing?" I said. "This is exactly what Jesus has been telling me."

For by grace you have been saved through faith and not of yourself; it is the gift of God, not of works, lest anyone can boast. For we are His workmanship, created in Christ Jesus for good works. Ephesians Chpt. 2:8-9,

My first reaction to reading these words was; "Good! That means we don't have to volunteer to mow the lawn, babysit the pastor's kids, scrub the kitchen floor or wash windows at the church. Someone who still believes they are saved by good works can do that." Then I read verse 10. *For we are His workmanship, created in Christ Jesus for good works.* So I may have to undergo a little attitude adjustment.

I started underlining the verses in the Bible that applied to me. Reading in Philippians 2:4, NKJ *Let each of you look out not only for his own interests, but also for the interests of others, and* verse 14: *Do all things without murmuring and disputing.* Wherever I turned in the New Testament the verses applied to me. Philippians 3:17 *Forget those things which are behind and reach forward to those things which are ahead.*

It wasn't long until the Bible that had been sitting on the shelf unused for years showed signs of wear, and it was extensively underlined. I even bought a couple of other versions and was amazed how much easier they were to read while retaining the same meaning.

The conclusion I reached after a month of study was that; God does speak directly to me through the scripture. It's like He is walking beside me giving me this message:

"You have a job to do looking after others; do it without mumbling and grumbling. Forget what has happened and move on. I'm here for you. Talk to me. If you can do this the peace of God which surpasses all understanding will guard your heart and mind through Christ Jesus. You can do all things through Christ who strengthens you. Learn to be content in whatever life hands you."

Wow!! That pretty much sums up what I need to do and identifies the source of my help. My job here on earth is to take up my cross daily and follow Jesus just like He told me earlier.

God gave me the special gift of the Holy Spirit, but it's up to me now to determine what I will do with that gift. When the cart-paths of life become bumpy, how am I going to remember to reach down into the depths of my heart and pull out my newly acquired faith? How will the Spirit respond when the going gets tough?

Out on the highways and byways of life I found that everywhere I looked God was giving me gentle reminders. While driving one day with my little grandsons in the back seat, we passed by a man hoeing in his garden.

"Look gramma, that man hoes and waters his garden every day, look how big his corn is." Preston said.

Won't my faith grow tall if I feed and water it every day by reading God's Word and taking time to pray?

Each Spring in the pasture across the street from our house, the wild flowers and new yucca sprouts burst into bloom and the new colts prance around on wobbly legs. It reminds me of the beautiful spring day that I decided to follow Jesus.

I know now that God never closes a door without opening a window. My sister Carol died while down the hall a new grandson was being born.

Two days later we received a call that Cork's brother-in-law who had lung cancer was not expected to live very long. As soon as Carol's funeral was over we drove to Albuquerque to say our good-byes to him, and spend time with Rose and her family. Felton was one of the intellectual types. He wanted to talk and he wanted answers to questions. There wasn't time to call in an expert.

"Why are we put here on Earth? What is our purpose in life?

Even with my new found faith in God I didn't feel qualified to answer. But I told him what I believed. "I feel we were put on earth to multiply and spread the word of God's Kingdom, to glorify God and enjoy Him forever and to take up our cross daily and follow Jesus." The words flowed from my mouth and again I wasn't sure where they came from.

"If that's true," he said, "We have failed miserably."

"Yes," I answered, "We have failed miserably, but you have asked for forgiveness. Jesus is waiting for you in heaven."

In the fall we loaded our motorhome and drove to Missouri and spent a few days visiting with my sister Mary, who was struggling with cancer. We drove on to Tennessee and planned to return when she was scheduled for surgery the next week. I couldn't help worrying. No matter how much faith I had I knew deep down in my heart that my little sister was going to die too. One day we passed by a little church with a sign out front reading, "Do what you can and trust God to do the rest." Another of God's gentle reminders.

We drove on into Tennessee, where I convinced my traveling companions to attend a non-denominational church where they were celebrating World Wide Communion Day. Children presenting the bread were dressed in costumes from other parts of the world. Each plate had several different kinds of bread originating in other countries. The Lord's prayer was repeated in Hungarian, Spanish, Portuguese, German, and Dutch. What an impressive way to emphasize World Wide Communion. God was reminding us that even though there are many different denominations with various religious beliefs we can all come together in worship and praise to celebrate communion. God's way of reminding me that we are all the same no matter what our background.

In the pastor's message that morning he said, "We are not to think we are better than anyone else." I wondered if that applied to me when on Sunday mornings I pass by a man out mowing his lawn. Doesn't he know how very much he's missing by not being in church? Am I not better than he is because I know Jesus? No doubt God is giving me a gentle reminder that sharing my faith with others will increase the number of people who know Him. Using my new training could help balance the ratio between the unchurched, lightlychurched and Christians. I also need to remember that each person can be at a different level in his/her faith journey. And it's not my place to judge whether the man mowing his lawn on Sunday morning is a Christian..

It reminded me of our pastor's words in the sermon just before we left home, "Everyone is to work out their salvation in their own way." That's why we have so many different churches. One of the joys of being American is that we are free to worship God in our own way. Sometimes it takes a while for the words of a sermon to soak into my foggy brain. I have often left church wondering to myself, "Just what did he/she mean by that?" Then later I get these gentle reminders that start me pondering again.

Continuing our journey we attended a Tennessee Mountain Homecoming near Knoxville. It was like traveling back in time 100 years. A way the Tennessee mountain folk choose to preserve their heritage.

As we walked around the small Tennessee village I heard music coming from a little church and I strolled inside. The church was holding an all-day hymn-singing. I waited for someone to leave before finding a spot on a rough-hewn log bench. I bowed my head in prayer while mountain folk played the old hymns on a violin and banjo. I soon joined in the singing. "Give Me That Old Time Religion" and "Amazing Grace" played with a hoe-down, mountain beat, soon had everyone clapping their hands and bouncing with joy. A spine-tingling, inspirational experience. It filled my heart with joy because I knew Jesus. Another of God's gentle reminders.

We headed back to Missouri to be with Mary, stopping at my brother Dale's small farm near Springfield before continuing on to Columbia, where Mary was in a cancer hospital. On the front door of Dale's house was a note. "Dale fell off a ladder and broke his shoulder. He is in a Springfield hospital."

What else could go wrong? "Seems like the devil is still busy. I thought we left him in Nebraska," I told my husband as we drove to the Springfield hospital. Dale was to be released the next day and had a friend lined up to help him. That afternoon we drove to Columbia, only to find Mary in a coma.

"Mary, talk to me," I said. She didn't respond, hadn't eaten for two days and the nurses blamed cancer, with too many chemo treatments and collapsed veins.

"She won't live long," the nurse told me and left the room.

I sat there helplessly and prayed while still trying to rouse her. I didn't want her to die. I hadn't had a chance to talk with her and to tell her Jesus loved her. All of a sudden I remembered how my sister Carol acted when she went into a diabetic coma. I called the nurse and insisted they take Mary's blood sugar. I couldn't believe, knowing she was diabetic, it hadn't been tested in three days.

After the results of the blood test the RN came in and administered insulin. Within ten minutes Mary was awake and talking to me. The next day the nurse received a reprimand. I could hear it clear down the hall. She had ordered the blood test and administered the insulin without a doctor's order. This angel of mercy saved my sisters life and I told her supervisor so. God was using the nurse and me to carry out His plan for Mary's life. It wasn't time for Mary to die. She hadn't made her peace with God. Before we left for home I took the time to share my faith with Mary, pray for her and convince her that Jesus loved her, forgave her and was waiting for her. That was in October. Mary lived until March. Before Mary's death I took my mother and traveled again to Missouri spending a week. Every day mom and I grew closer to the Lord, to Mary and to each other as we prayed with her and shared her last few days.

I praise God every day and thank him for the time He has allowed me to spend with my family and friends before their deaths. **Although it is unpleasant**, it touches my heart deeply and assures me that one day I will see them all again.

As time goes on God's many gentle reminders and a deepening faith will carry me through whatever life hands me. Including keeping the devil away from my door.

Chapter Eighteen

THE GAME OF LIFE

As I wrote the last chapter of *Jesus In My Golf Cart*, another friend had just passed away. As God closed this door he opened another window for Betty's family. On the same day Betty died, her twin great grandchildren were born premature. One twin died but the other seems to have Betty's spirit. He's a fighter.

At the funeral I shared this story with Betty's family about our friendship.

I first met Betty at the bowling alley in the early 60's. We never bowled on the same team but I was always opposite her in the lineup. I secretly hoped she didn't make her spare and she held her breath, hoping I wouldn't get a double that meant a win for my team. Many times at the end of the year our teams finished first and second in the standings. We were both better than average bowlers and took our games seriously.

Our three sons were the same age as two of her boys, which led us to the Little League ball park. This meant that most of the time our families were cheering against each other.

Then we both joined a women's softball league, playing on seperate teams. The intense rivalry that built up at the bowling alley carried over to softball. Our team members screamed with joy every time I caught a high fly to left field off from Betty's bat. And members of her team cheered when they stopped my line drive and turned it into a double play.

The years traveled by much too fast. The kids grew up and our bodies rebelled against softball.

Betty quit bowling when she and Carl moved to Louisiana for a short time. I replaced Betty on the team I had cheered against for many years. Then I took up golf and eventually quit bowling.

Betty and Carl returned to Kimball to retire and attended our church one day with son Mike and his family. It was good to see Betty. I welcomed her with a hug (our first ever) and invited them to come back again. Later that week I called and invited her to a women's meeting at the church.

Then we both signed up for an exercise class. On the days we didn't exercise we walked three miles. We vented our frustrations about husbands, kids, and life in general, while trying to shed a few ounces.

I helped convince Betty and Carl to join the church and attended instruction classes with them. We learned more about what was expected of a Christian and asked a lot of questions about theology. Our knowledge increased, and as we studied the Bible we grew closer to our Lord Jesus Christ.

Through this experience Betty and I became good friends. There was no longer a need to be rivals. **For the first time we were playing on the same team**. Jesus was our captain and reminded us often that it doesn't matter whether you win or lose...It's how you play the game.. Betty lost the game of life, but died peacefully...knowing Jesus was waiting for her.

After reading this eulogy I thought about all the games I've played throughout life and how serious and important each one seemed at the time. I was a strong competitor. It was my whole life. Better than average sports ability, material possesions; ball glove and bat, the best bowling ball and shoes available, golf cart and top of the line clubs, with designer clothes to match, don't mean a thing when the Doctor's diagnosis is cancer or some other life-threatening disease...The only thing that matters is whether I'm walking and talking with Jesus.

EPILOGUE

Making the decision to follow Jesus didn't remove the devil from my life. It didn't immediately cure cancer and a worn out heart for my younger sisters. It didn't keep my parents from aging and needing more and more attention. It didn't remove the stress of everyday life and running a business. I did discover that the golf course is open Sunday afternoons, as well as morning, and the gate won't have to be closed if I'm not there every day.

Decreasing my time at the golf course becomes easier as muscles grow weaker from post-polio syndrome and fibromyalgia. At the same time I have discovered new talents. I didn't realize I could write anything until I started my walk with Jesus. Writing, visiting the elderly and enjoying grandsons, now fill the empty hours when rest becomes a necessity and golf takes a back seat along with BUB.

Walking with Jesus lightened my burden and helped me learn to deal with elderly parents, their care and eventual death. The Spirit filled me with strength and comforting words to say while sharing my faith through the illness and death of an aunt, two sisters, my parents, a brother- in-law, and several dear friends. The newly learned lessons about love, patience and forgiveness have enhanced my relationship with my family and friends.

I've learned that forgiveness and love are necessary in a church family too. I can't have the Spirit in my heart and still harbor resentment. For the first time I noticed the sign that hangs over the entrance to our church. ***"Servants Entrance"*** As one pastor reminded us not long ago, We are all to be ministers. It didn't happen for me until I accepted the gift of the the Holy Spirit.

In the book *Mere Christianity*, C.S. Lewis says, "Putting on Christ is not one among many jobs a Christian has to do; and it is not a sort of special exercise for the top class. It is the whole of Christianity. Christianity offers nothing else at all."

How else can I "put on Christ" without taking Him with me every day? I need to put Jesus on every morning like well worn jeans and sneakers. The full armor of God, Father, Son and Holy Spirit, are available to help the fight against Beelzebub. When I am tempted, God in three persons helps me to remember my values and meet the challenge.

Last week I received this little story from a friend over e-mail.

A lady had recently been baptized. One of her co-workers asked her what it was like to be a Christian. She was caught off guard and didn't know how to answer, but when she looked up she saw a jack-o'-lantern on the desk and answered:

"It's like being a pumpkin. God picks you from the patch and brings you in and washes off all the dirt on the outside that you got from being around all the other pumpkins. Then he cuts off the top and takes all the yucky stuff out from inside. He removes all those seeds of doubt, hate, greed, etc. Then he carves you a new smiling face and puts his light inside of you to shine for all to see." **Author Unknown.**

There's still a few seeds and yucky stuff left in me. **I am a work in progress**. Depression at times keeps my light from shining as bright as it should. On days when smiling doesn't come easy it helps to sit down and share my sense of humor on paper. Thanks for reading *Jesus In My Golf Cart.*

SNOWBIRD MATING SEASON

Bernita Jackson Brown
Illustrated by Paul Winer

Snowbird Mating Season

by

Bernita Brown
Illustrated by Paul Winer.

It was 6:30 pm as we rolled down Interstate 10, five miles east of our destination. The blaring CB radio was tuned to channel 19. All of a sudden a confused trucker sounded off loud and clear, "What in the hell's going on here? I came through Quartzsite a couple of months ago and this town was deader than a squashed lizard. Look at all the campers, there must be thousands of RVs."

Haven't you heard came the cheerful reply, "It's Snowbird Mating Season."

Snowbird Mating Season is a humorous account of how a seemingly dead town in summer is revitalized and brimming with flavor as Snowbirds (Retired People) from across the U.S. and Canada converge on southwest Arizona in the winter, bringing their nests (RVs) with them. Where do they go? What do they do? Let Bernita's keen sense of humor and Paul Winer's illustrations entertain you. Second updated edition coming to you from 1st Books Library-Fall 2001

Limited amount of first edition available from:

Snowbird Publishing
3261 Rd.43
Kimball, NE 69145
snowbird@megavision.com

The largest segment of our population is nearing retirement age. Many are choosing the RV way of life while searching for the ideal spot for winter nesting. Other's are RVing full time. How do you retire and live on a fixed income? Where do they go? What do they do cooped up in a small RV for months at a time.

Snowbird Mating Season is written especially for and about those who love the RV way of life. A fine synopsis of what life is like in Southwest Arizona, during *Snowbird Mating Season* An excellent gift for your soon-to-be retiring friends.

Bernita Brown and Paul Winer's first book together.

ABOUT THE AUTHOR

Bernita Jackson Brown, born and raised in the small Western Nebraska town of Kimball, is often called Nebraska's Erma Bombeck. She started writing at the age of *50* after raising her three sons. Bernita and husband Noia (Cork) Brown run a water well drilling and repair business. After many trips running parts and assisting in her family business Bernita wrote her first humor article and had it published in Water Well Journal She is the author of the book Snowbird Mating Season, a humorous story about snowbirds (retired people) who fly south for the winter, taking their nests (RVs) with them. Bernita has been published in various publications and now writes for RVCompanion. Although Bernita likes to write humor she is very serious about her walk with Christ and her fellowship with the Holy Spirit as portrayed in her new book A Stranger In My Golf Cart.

The empty space in my golf cart is reserved for you.

CPSIA information can be obtained
at www.ICGtesting.com
Printed in the USA
LVHW011524060521
686701LV00002B/505